PHOENIX PARK

PHOENIX PARK

A History and Guidebook

Brendan Nolan

The Liffey Press

Published by
The Liffey Press
Ashbrook House, 10 Main Street
Raheny, Dublin 5, Ireland
www.theliffeypress.com

ISBN 1-904148-78-6

"Beacons at Bealtaine" on page 123 © Seamus Heaney,
published with the kind permission of the poet

Printed in Spain by GraphyCems.

CONTENTS

ABOUT THE AUTHOR

 Brendan Nolan has reported on Phoenix Park as a freelance journalist for several decades and was a professional observer at many of the events of the late twentieth century related herein. He was born in Chapelizod in a house beside the churchyard of Le Fanu and counted Phoenix Park as his personal rambling ground through his growing years and beyond. He is married with two sons and three grandchildren, thus far. Brendan is webmaster for www.liffey-i.com, a local website that includes stories and updates on Phoenix Park.

Acknowledgements

Thanks for freely given support and assistance to: Maurice Ahern, William Barton, Elizabeth Buckley, Joe Buggy, Hugh Bonnar, Doreen and Paddy Bray, Tom Burke, Nuala Canny, Margaret Connolly, Don Doran, Owen Farrelly, Eddie Fitzgerald, Margaret Gormley, Niall Hatch, Mark Hogan, Cian Kenny, John and Zena Lamont, Brian Langan, Ned Lee, Pat Liddy, Jim Manning and three generations of Mannings who were rangers, John McCullen, Garda Sergeant Pat McGee, Kenneth McGowan, Margaret McGuirk, George Moir, Gráinne Mooney, Anthony Morrissey, Bridget Noble, Rita, Rory and Kevin Nolan, Pearse Street library staff, Charlie O'Leary, Padraic O'Farrell, Colette O'Flaherty, Bróna Olwill, Tony Roche, Robert Wiggens.

Image Credits

The author and publishers wish to thank the following individuals and organisations for kind permission to reproduce their copyrighted photographs and illustrations: © National Library of Ireland: front cover top, pages 8, 12, 16, 20, 148; © Office of Public Works: pages 28, 36, 37, 41, 43, 47, 71, 73, 77, 80, 99, 133, 136, 137, 139, 150, 154, 159, 192, 195, 202, 208, 210, 212, 214, 220, 228; © John McCullen/OPW: pages 62, 63, 64, 65, 67, 152, 153, 156, 189, 193, 196; © Dublin Zoo: pages 177, 179, 185; © Garda Museum: pages 81, 91, 93, 95; © Pat Liddy: pages 4, 60, 74, 181, 223, 226; © Pat Langan/*The Irish Times*: front cover bottom, page 122; © Eddie Kelly/*The Irish Times*: page 84; © Dave Mulholland: page 53; © Irish Motor Racing Club Archives: pages 168, 171; © Rita Nolan: pages 30, 51, 78, 201, 230; © Brian Langan: pages 198, 225; Courtesy of Jim Manning: pages 84, 87.

For May and Jem and all that followed thereafter

INTRODUCTION

Phoenix Park has been a part of Dublin and Ireland since the seventeenth century and is set fair for continued enjoyment and relaxation into the twenty-first century. It has been home to diverse species, ranging from wandering man to the busy ants that help to spread the furze bush seeds that created the Furry Glen, a protected area situated in the heart of what is now the wilderness area of Phoenix Park.

Princes, presidents and paupers have passed the night in the park; some have enjoyed their stay, some came to harm, some sadly even lost their lives. Their spirits, perhaps, may haunt the park to this day. Such possibilities have given spur over the centuries to the imaginations of writers who have used the park as a setting for horrid ghost stories. Such stories are easily dismissed in daylight but may be rekindled if one has occasion to cross the park in darkness, when an unexpected sound might prompt a moment of terror and cause the breath to catch in the throat.

The park is a large enclosed area of 1,752 acres and within its walls are to be found both passive and active recreational facilities. Phoenix Park has a rich architectural heritage; if one were to trace a trail from one building to the next, a necklace of wonder would emerge. No two buildings in the park have the same design. Some, like the lodges in Áras an Uachtaráin, the home of the President carry older names like the Henman's Lodge or the Cowman's Lodge to recall their former use in the life of the park.

Phoenix Park was the home of the three most powerful men in Ireland under British rule: the Lord Lieutenant, the Chief Secretary and the Under Secretary. It is home now to the President of Ireland and the Ambassador of the United States. The Phoenix Park Visitor Centre was also a residence, until a few years ago, to the Papal Nuncio, the representative of the Vatican in Ireland.

Behind high railings, the park houses the headquarters of the Garda Síochána, the national police force, and quietly sitting in the southeast corner is the headquarters of the Defence Forces. There is a major hospital in the park at St Mary's that, in different incarnations, sheltered the orphaned and abandoned children of British soldiers and in later times played its part in the war against TB. It now caters for an elderly population of patients.

For sports people there are organised games and activities and spaces allotted to particular pastimes and there are wide open expanses for others engaged in solitary sports. For lovers there are paths and woods to explore as a life together beckons, and for families there are the myriad wonders of Dublin Zoo with which to while away the hours.

On summer Sundays, there is free music on the Victorian bandstand in the Hollow or in the newly reopened Farmleigh, and a ramble through the park will nearly always reveal some other activity in progress to marvel at or take part in.

For the future, there is a five-year development plan in hand that strives to protect the park for its inhabitants and its users. Once a suburb of Dublin city and a place to escape to from the smoky city, Phoenix Park faces modern pressures undreamt of in the 1600s when it was first conceived of as a royal deer park. Most pressure comes from commuter interests and public representatives wishing to open the park to yet more commuter traffic on the way to somewhere else. By the turn of the twenty-first century some 30,000 motor cars were using the park as an access route every day, causing major pollution and no little frustration to other park users. Public transport is not allowed to use the park, but as pressure grows on outside roads from new housing estates in the hinterland, continuing demands are made by politicians of every hue to allow buses to use the park as a clearway into and out of Dublin — hardly a use compatible with a public oasis of calm in the middle of a capital city.

Most likely, the park will prevail as it has always done, as a park for people and for wildlife. Dublin author and historian Eamon Mac Thomáis, who was himself a lover of all things Dublin, speaking at the opening of the Strawberry Fair on the Strawberry Beds in 1995, said:

> When you start in a Dublin life you take your first steps in the Flower Gardens in the Park, then at six years or so you go to the Monument, and then the cricket grounds with coats as goalposts, then on to the camogie pitches to watch girls, up to the pitches to play football and then, with your girlfriend, on to the Furry Glen and the Strawberry Beds. Birth to Grave in the park . . .

Phoenix Park is and always has been Dublin's own Pleasure Gardens.

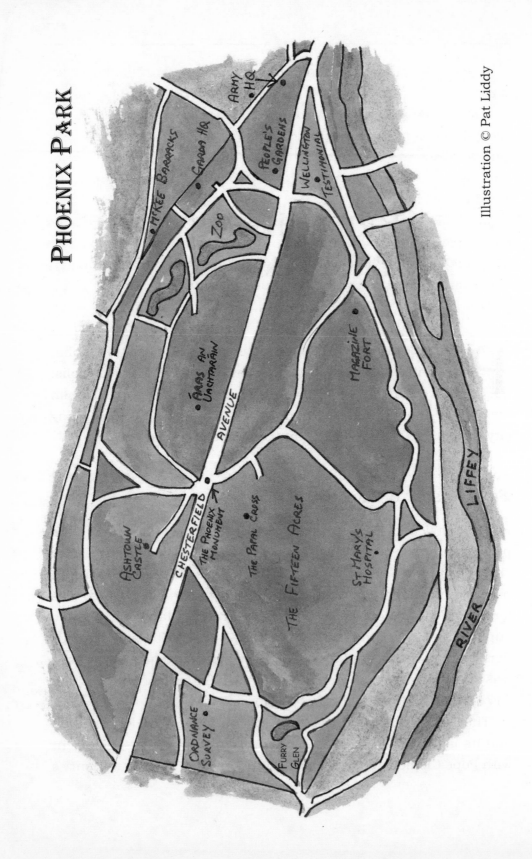

Phoenix Park

Illustration © Pat Liddy

A Brief History of Phoenix Park

Phoenix Park lies both within and without the city of Dublin. When its walls were built, they lay outside of the metropolis, but it did not take long before the park became a part of Dublin life. Today, though now surrounded on all sides by the expanding city, it remains both a part of and apart from the capital.

Fionn Uisce to Phoenix

Events outside its 1,752 walled acres have shaped and affected the park through the centuries. Not the least of these were the Christian crusades to the Holy Land in the Middle Ages. To defend Christian pilgrims en route, a fighting order, the Knights Hospitaller, was formed. Wealthy donors gave the Order tracts of land in Ireland to support its work. Lands at Kilmainham and what became Phoenix Park were part of a land grant made by Strongbow in 1174, which was subsequently passed to the Knights of St John of Jerusalem in 1177 by Hugh Tyrell, First Baron of Castleknock.

The Order was suppressed in the turmoil of the Reformation and its lands seized in 1537 by Henry VIII, after his disagreement with Pope Clement VII over the dissolution of yet another of Henry's marriages. Some of the lands were leased to Sir Edward Fisher, who in 1611 built a country residence on St Thomas' Hill, later the Magazine Hill, overlooking the Liffey Valley and with views towards the city. The house was called "The Phoenix", and it is there that the name for the park seems to have originated. The area had a spring of clear water, which in Irish would be *fionn uisce*; "phoenix" would be a near-enough anglicisation of this. The name remained, apparently with no other association with the mythical bird that arises whole from its own ashes.

Fisher was not long in possession when, in 1616, the government of the day acquired the land and house from him on payment of £2,500. The house became the official residence of the Irish Viceroys. (The Lord Lieutenant or Viceroy, from the French *vice roi* or "deputy king", ruled Ireland for the English crown.) However, just ten years later, the Viceroys decamped two miles to Chapelizod House and remained there for the next hundred years or thereabouts. Meanwhile, Fisher's house on the hill fell into decay.

James Butler, the Duke of Ormond, was appointed Lord Lieutenant or Viceroy in 1644 by Charles I; but Ormond surrendered Dublin to Oliver Cromwell in 1647 in the English Civil War then raging between royalists and parliamentarians. The execution of Charles I in 1649 ended the Civil War, and Ormond's job.

Incidentally, the gallows for public executions within the County of Dublin stood on ground now occupied by Parkgate Street, where the main entrance to the park now lies. In 1646, the gallows was moved to a new location at Kilmainham to make room for building at the park gates.

BUILDING THE PARK

In May 1660 Charles II was restored to the throne, and Ormond was re-appointed Lord Lieutenant, a position he took up in 1661. Determined to develop the Phoenix area as a park, Ormond introduced deer, partridge and pheasant onto the lands. Two military officers were sent to England to purchase and transport deer back to Dublin. Another envoy was sent to North Wales to trap partridge; and in County Wicklow the Earl of Ossory captured pheasants on his father's estate near Arklow for the stocking of Phoenix Park in 1662. However, it was soon found that deer were straying and fowl were being poached, so a perimeter wall was commissioned to encompass the lands.

The following year, William Dodson began the erection of the wall, a job that was to continue into 1664. He was paid £6,000 for his efforts. The custom of the time was to build something and count the cost afterwards. Dodson was apparently advanced cash-on-demand as he required it. Unfortunately, as Dodson completed the wall, it was found to be broken in a dozen different places. The erstwhile contractor claimed that severe weather had caused the damage but, according to an official inquiry, unsuitable stone was used and bad workmanship in construction meant that parts of the wall were falling down on a daily basis. The gaps were filled with furze and thorns.

Undeterred, Dodson offered to keep the walls in repair for £100 a year and then attempted to sub-let the contract to his own workers for £30 a year. It became obvious that a Dodson wall would not stand and another solution would have to be sought.

Six years later, in 1671, Ormond bought and added the Phoenix and Newtown Lands for £3,000, on a royal mandate in trust for Charles II. With the building of the Royal Hospital at Kilmainham, which commenced in 1680, the park was reduced to its present size of 1,752 acres, and a new wall was commissioned.

Up to this time, the park had extended on both sides of the River Liffey up as far as Kilmainham and out to Chapelizod and it was decided to make the Chapelizod Road the southern boundary, effectively removing the river from the park's area of concern. In 1680, a new wall was constructed by Sir John Temple, Solicitor General of Ireland, in exchange for £200 and a tract of land between

An early nineteenth-century engraving showing a view of Dublin city from Phoenix Park (©National Library of Ireland)

the wall on Chapelizod Road and the river. Temple built the wall to the satisfaction of all.

In response to a continuing loss of animals, three keepers were appointed to the park, one of whom was superior to the others and held the title of Ranger. These were men of high position who delegated their work to subordinates. However, defective walls, vermin and poachers did not make for an easy job, and the matter was made more difficult when the poachers were discovered to be mainly soldiers from the Dublin garrisons. Apparently Charles II's concern for pleasing people, and his lady friends in particular, did not extend to ensuring his soldiery had enough to eat!

Not long established, the park faced a crisis in the 1670s when, during the viceroyalty of Essex, Charles II sought to give the park to his mistress, the Duchess of Cleveland; but while the King was in favour of the transfer to the Duchess's estates, Essex and Ormond joined forces to prevent it, much to the good lady's annoyance.

As time passed and the city grew, the park became a popular place to ride out to from the city to watch hawks chase prey across the grasslands. By the turn of the century, hundreds of people were regularly to be seen on horseback pursuing the hawks for a better view of the chase.

THE EIGHTEENTH CENTURY

Phoenix House, by now in decay, was pulled down as the eighteenth century dawned, and in 1735 a magazine was built for the storage of arms and explosives for the Dublin regiments. This was to be the century of armed revolution in many countries, including France, the United States and Ireland. Military reviews were conducted on the Fifteen Acres as part of the garrisoning of Dublin. Indeed, as a schoolboy, in the 1770s, Dubliner Theobald Wolfe Tone, who later founded the United Irishmen with Thomas Russell and Napper Tandy, played truant from school and watched the military reviews in Phoenix Park. The military reviews were popular affairs and in 1780, 100,000 people gathered on the Fifteen Acres to review the Irish Volunteers (Province of Leinster). (See Chapter 4 for more on the park's military links.)

Apart from military matters, the park enjoyed great renown as a fashionable place of recreation. In fair weather in the early decades of the eighteenth century, many strollers frequented a clearing in the middle of a wood described as "the resort of belle and beaux" in contemporary reports. The wood was interspersed with glades. However, in 1731, Lord Chesterfield (Philip Downes Stanhope), the serving Lord Lieutenant, swept the clearing away when he laid out a garden with plants and walls and erected the Phoenix Column in the centre of what had been the clearing. He placed a phoenix atop the column, continuing the misreading of *fionn uisce*.

In 1745, the park was officially opened to the public and Chesterfield planted chestnuts and elms along the central avenue, which now bears his name. In 1754, less than ten years after public access to the park was granted, Park Ranger Nathaniel Clements began construction of the house that was to become home to Ireland's rulers until independence in 1922. On the establishment of the Irish Free State it became the home of the Governor General. In 1938, Douglas Hyde took up residence as the first Irish President. Today it is maintained as Áras an Uachtaráin, home to the President of Ireland. Newtown Lodge, as it was first called, was built on the site of an earlier building, with a rolling view of the Dublin mountains to the south. It was flanked by trees planted by Chesterfield, many of which still stand today. The house was sold to the government for £25,000 and, as the Vice Regal Lodge, became the official residence of the Viceroys. Some royal appointees were more active in the post than others. The Chief Secretary administered the country with his staff from Dublin Castle, under the Lord Lieutenant. The original Newtown Lodge may have been home to the Ranger and keeper of the Newtown Walk, which was incorporated into Phoenix Park.

In 1772, Sir John Blaquiere was named Bailiff of Phoenix Park and received a four-roomed cottage, which he extended into a Georgian house on sixty acres. The house is now home to the serving United States' Ambassador. It was completed in 1776 and six years later the Government bought it for £7,000 from Blaquiere as an official residence for the Chief Secretary of Ireland. Before this, however, there was an obstacle to be overcome. Lawyer Napper Tandy, one of the founders of the United Irishmen, who would rise in armed rebellion in 1798, challenged Blaquiere in a Dublin court following the latter's annexation of some thirty acres of the park for his new residence. The court found in Blaquiere's favour on the land grab while delivering a ruling on ownership and use of the park by everybody else. The court stated:

> It was only by leave of the King the citizens had liberty to recreate themselves under restrictions such as not riding on cars, not bringing in dogs or guns, and not sending their servants to air their horses during the fencing month.

In the course of the case, Blaquiere was called the King's Cowboy by the plaintiffs, a name that stuck. The following appeared in the *Freeman's Journal* shortly afterwards.

Blaquiere's Triumph

Immersed in fogs,
These stubborn dogs,
Their stinking streets may trail,

Who rashly tried,
So late with pride
Their master's right assail

Debarred the roads,
Near our abodes,
No car no coach shall pass.

Our cows alone
(The soil's our own)
Shall eat the Royal grass

"Ho" cries Blaquiere
"I may now sneer
At every patriot jury

Black Philip strained.
My cause I gained
In spite of all their fury

Is Dublin free?
Her bane I'll be,
Linked with my three

Partakers
The 'King's Cowboy',
I'll now enjoy the precious acres.

By George preferred,
To guard his herd,
No citizen shall dare —

> So late subdued
> The Park intrude
> For exercise and air."

However, many seem to have ignored the king and his courts because, by 1779, the *Freeman's Journal* was complaining that games of hurling were being allowed in Phoenix Park on Sunday evenings.

On 14 March 1792, some 10,000 journeymen, artificers, apprentices and labourers assembled on the Nine Acres, beside the polo grounds, to protest against the Combination Laws. Subsequently passed, the Combination Acts forbade amalgamations of persons for the purpose of political reform. Interference with commerce and trade became illegal. The government, unsurprisingly, saw wage claims as a clear sign of disaffection. This was against the background of the French Revolution which began in 1789 and upended the old order there, and subsequently across many other countries.

The Irish Rising of 1798 saw troops stationed in Phoenix Park and its nearby barracks being used to face the rebels in battle in the risen areas of County Wexford and elsewhere as the rebellion descended into atrocity and reprisal on both sides. Charles Cornwallis, the English general who had surrendered at Yorktown to the Patriot

The main entrance to Phoenix Park at the beginning of the twentieth century (©National Library of Ireland, Lawrence Collection Royal 6167)

forces to end the successful American War of Independence, was appointed Viceroy in 1798. He was also named Commander-in-Chief of the army, in order to deal with the Irish rebellion. Cornwallis restrained the worst of the bloody reprisals of the crown forces and attempted to bring about some reconciliation. Among the revolutionaries taken prisoner following the crushing of the Rising was the same Theobald Wolfe Tone who had watched the military reviews in the Phoenix Park; he would later die in captivity.

Two years later, the Irish Parliament voted itself out of office following widespread corruption and bribery of the sitting deputies. In 1801, the Act of Union brought Ireland into a political union with Great Britain.

The Nineteenth Century

Five years after the Union was agreed, the Dublin-born Arthur Wellesley was appointed Chief Secretary for Ireland and served until 1809, having already been an Irish MP in the now defunct parliament. Later, as the Duke of Wellington, he commanded the forces that defeated Napoleon at Waterloo in 1815. He became Prime Minister of the United Kingdom in 1825, and four years later oversaw the passing of the Catholic Emancipation Act which restored rights long denied to the Catholic majority on the island.

The nineteenth century saw a drawn-out process of building a £20,000 monument to Wellington, to commemorate his military victories. Begun in 1817, it was finally completed on the site of the salute battery in Phoenix Park some forty years later. At sixty-three metres high, it was the world's tallest obelisk then, and was second only to the Washington Memorial's 169 metres for many years. The Spire on Dublin's O'Connell Street, unveiled in 2003, stands at 120 metres in height. (See Chapter 3 for more on the Wellington monument and the other monuments in the park.)

The nineteenth century saw the most extensive development of the Phoenix Park. Some few years after the Napoleonic Wars ended, and the prospect of a French invasion of Ireland had receded, the Ordnance Survey took up residence in the park, in Mountjoy Barracks, in 1824. Dublin Zoo opened its gates in 1831. In 1842, a police depot was built in the north-eastern corner of Phoenix Park, for recruiting and training the Irish Constabulary, which had been formed in 1836. They were later granted the prefix Royal for suppressing the 1867 Fenian Rising, yet another armed rebellion against British rule. The RIC was replaced in 1922, on independence, by the Garda Síochána, or Civic Guard, of the new state, but they retained their headquarters in the park (see Chapter 4).

A mains gas supply arrived from the city in 1852, providing street lighting and gas supply to the Vice Regal Lodge and to the park's roads. The Office of Public Works took over responsibility for the park and its buildings in 1860, a duty it continues to fulfil to the present day.

The People's Flower Gardens were laid out in 1864 beside the park gates and opposite the recently completed Wellington monument. A few years later, the monument, by then a focal point of meetings and other activities, witnessed a police charge against 5,000 people attending an 1871 Fenian amnesty meeting (see Chapter 7).

When John Winston Spencer-Churchill, the Duke of Marlborough, was appointed Viceroy in 1876, his son Lord Randolph Churchill arrived in Dublin as his Private Secretary. Randolph lived with his family in the Private Secretary's Lodge and his son Winston Churchill roamed the Vice Regal gardens as a small child, reportedly driving happily along the wide paths on a donkey and cart. He recalled witnessing his grandfather talking loudly to a crowd gathered for the unveiling of the Lord Gough equestrian statue in 1878, which was to last less than eighty years, being blown up by nationalists in 1957.

A few years after the arrival of Britain's future wartime leader, the national revival of hurling began in Phoenix Park (though there was no connection between the two events!). The Dublin Hurling Club was formed in 1882 by a group of men including Michael Cusack. While the early hurling club was to fail, it provided an impetus that led to the forming of the GAA in Thurles, County Tipperary, eighteen months later on 1 November 1884, with Michael Cusack as its first General Secretary.

That same year, Cusack resumed hurling sessions in Phoenix Park and play continued each weekend. Games by then were being played at the Wellington Monument and spectators were encouraged to join in the matches, so it's anybody's guess how many people were chasing one small ball at any given time across the park!

Ball games were all the rage in those years and in September 1890 Bohemian Football Club was founded at a meeting in Phoenix Park. It too played its games of soccer on the Nine Acres. Indeed, when the players finished a match, they carried the goalposts to the gate lodge at the North Circular Road entrance for safe storage.

On the darker side, there were more dangerous times ahead for those residing in Phoenix Park. On 6 May 1887, at a spot quite near the Nine Acres, two men were stabbed to death in an action that was to have widespread repercussions for the government of Ireland and the Home Rule movement of the time.

Earl Spencer, the new Viceroy, arrived in Dublin on 6 May 1887, accompanied by a new Chief Secretary, Lord Frederick Cavendish. Following a meeting in Dublin Castle, Spencer left for the Vice Regal Lodge accompanied by a mounted escort. Cavendish, who knew Dublin well, walked to Phoenix Park. As Cavendish walked along, his Under Secretary, Thomas Burke, alighted from a cab to join him on the May evening stroll. A short time later, they were stabbed to death by political assailants and left lying beside the road while the killers made off towards Chapelizod. The killings were committed by members of the Invincibles, a small revolutionary nationalist group, six of whose members were hanged for the crime in Kilmainham the following year (see Chapter 5).

*Mounted constables on duty on Chesterfield Avenue
at the turn of the twentieth century
(©National Library of Ireland, New Series Collection 5674)*

THE TWENTIETH CENTURY

Some 3,000 trees of all species were blown down in the park during the great storm of 1903. The only other comparable loss of trees was in the 1980s when Dutch elm disease carried away 2,000 trees, many of them Lord Chesterfield's original plantings.

By this time, the motor car was established on Irish roads, and speed trials in 1903 saw the world land speed record being broken in Phoenix Park at speeds in excess of eighty-four miles per hour, at a time when a general speed limit of twenty miles per hour was in operation on public roads.

During the Easter Rising of 1916, getting out of Phoenix Park became difficult because of the hostilities in Dublin. At one stage, meat for feeding the animals in Dublin Zoo ran out. In order to keep the lions and tigers alive, some of the other animals in the zoo were killed and fed to the large cats, until a supply of horsemeat was secured.

On the first day of the Rising, Easter Monday 1916, 24 April, a party of thirty members of the Irish Volunteers and Fianna Éireann captured the Magazine Fort on St Thomas' Hill. They took guns and withdrew, after setting fires to blow up the magazine's ordinance, but the fuses burned out before reaching the ammunition and little damage was caused.

Rebels even had the audacity to shoot at the car of John Denton Pinkstone French, Commander of the British Home Forces and later the penultimate Lord Lieutenant of Ireland, when it was driving near the park gates. French was responsible for the suppression of the rising and the subsequent execution of the leaders at Kilmainham.

In 1918, French, the newly appointed Lord Lieutenant, brought military style to the Vice Regal Lodge as the War of Independence battled its way to the Anglo-Irish Treaty of 1921 that saw the eventual withdrawal of British forces from most of Ireland. French was eventually replaced, in 1921, by Viscount FitzAlan of Derwent, a Catholic, and the last of the Irish Viceroys. In 1922, the last Chief Secretary, Sir Harman Greenwood, departed Ireland.

As Saorstát Éireann, the Irish Free State, came into being, the Vice Regal Lodge served as the official residence of the Governors General, the crown's representatives in Ireland. Irish parliamentarian Tim Healy was appointed as the first Governor General of the Free State, and the house became his official residence. In 1937, a new Irish constitution provided that Ireland would have a President, known as Uachtarán na hÉireann, and an official residence, Áras an Uachtaráin, the former Vice Regal Lodge. It has been the official residence of the head of state since 1938. That year, Douglas Hyde was inaugurated as the first President of Ireland.

The new state was recognised by the United States when in 1927 the first US envoy to the Irish Free State, Frederick A. Sterling, opened a ministerial legation in Dublin. The former Chief Secretary's Lodge was rented from the OPW and until 1948 housed both the residence and the chancellery. In 1949, the post of Minister was changed to Ambassador and the United States itself took over the lease of the property in Phoenix Park.

In 1929, the centenary of Catholic Emancipation was celebrated by hundreds of thousands of people gathered on the Fifteen Acres. It was followed, in June 1932, by the Eucharistic Congress with even larger crowds in attendance, which in turn was followed by a papal mass in 1979 when almost one in three citizens of Ireland arrived in Phoenix Park on the same day to see Pope John Paul II celebrate mass. (These large-scale gatherings in the park are discussed in Chapter 7.)

EMERGENCY MEASURES

However, times were less happy during the Emergency, as the Second World War was called in neutral Ireland. Huge mounds of coal and turf were stored on the Fifteen Acres and on the Whitefields lands. The roads of the park became pitted and potholed from heavy truck use. The pressure of so much weight on soft ground affected the roots of mature trees along the main road, many of which succumbed to the stress on their root systems and died.

The weighbridge for the weighing of rationed fuel loaded by carriers was at Parkgate Street near where the public gallows had stood in earlier times, so all vehicles travelled up and down the same stretch of Chesterfield Avenue. One coal merchant, John Dowling of Blackpitts, recalled how on a freezing misty morning he sat atop a high load of turf while his brother Dick piloted their truck along the road. High and all as the load was, John recalled passing another motionless person in the mist sitting higher than he was. "I only realised afterwards that it was Gough on his statue. It's no wonder he didn't answer when I hailed him," said John.

Land was leased to Dublin Corporation for use as allotments during the Emergency and the deer herd was culled to about forty animals from some 800 during the severe winter of 1942. Plots were laid out on the Nine Acres and growers complained of the depredation caused by grazing sheep and wandering deer. The row reached the Dáil where the minister of the day referred representations from opposition politicians to the city corporation.

The European war was not long started when a convoy of IRA lorries removed load after load of stolen guns and ammunition in a cheeky raid on the Magazine Fort in the park on 23 December 1939. Lookouts were posted at the Islandbridge gates while a convoy of lorries was brought in to remove ammunition, rifles and machine-guns. However, such was the swift reaction of the defence forces that by 28 December, most of the stolen equipment had been recovered.

In May 1941, Dublin's North Strand was bombed and tensions rose as fears grew that this bombing was a prelude to an invasion by Germany. One bomb fell in Phoenix Park, beside the Dog Pond and the Phoenix Cricket Club. The blast reportedly shattered windows at Áras an Uachtaráin and the American Legation. The occupants of the pump house near the Dog Pond escaped injury but the house had to be demolished later. Buildings in the nearby Zoo were also damaged by the blast.

As Park Ranger Jim Manning recalled, such was the force of the explosion that even through the following day there was evidence of the incident: "There was smoke and dust everywhere. The pump house that was used to pump water up from lower levels for all the houses in the park was gone." The crater created beside the cricket club threw up so much debris that rocks fell through the clubhouse roof and the pitch was unplayable because of stones strewn across the surface. The club successfully claimed damages from the German government for its roof. Compensation totalling some £327,000 was received by the Minister for Finance from the Federal Republic of Germany after the war in respect of the bombing in the park and on North Strand. The final payment was made in 1958. The Zoo's damage bill came to £613.9s.3d.

RECENT MILESTONES

By the next decade, fireworks of a different kind were seen in Phoenix Park as part of An Tostál, a short-lived initiative to create a three-week long national festival in the weeks following Easter that would see people of Irish origin being welcomed home with an annual festival aimed at them.

In Seanad Éireann in June 1952, the Minister for Industry and Commerce Sean Lemass TD proposed investment in an open-air museum in Phoenix Park. "I think it would prove a great attraction for tourists. It would help our own people to realise how their fathers and grandfathers lived," he said. Years later, his nephew Noel Lemass TD, then in opposition, suggested such an open-air

The People's Flower Gardens around 1960
(©National Library of Ireland, Valentine Collection 2130)

museum should be located in the grounds of the Royal Hospital at Kilmainham. Nothing came of either suggestion.

By May 1958 political and military matters had quietened sufficiently in the park for questions to be asked in the Dáil about the ownership of weighing machines situated at the People's Gardens, and under whose authority they had been placed there. The machines in question, which for a penny would show a person's weight, were the property of the British Automatic Company Limited, their installation the subject of a licence granted by the Minister for Finance, following invitation of competitive offers.

In 1979, Pope John Paul II became arguably the most famous visitor to the park when he celebrated mass on the Fifteen Acres and visited President Paddy Hillery in Áras an Uachtaráin, planting a tree while he was there (see Chapter 7).

In June 1984, the Fifteen Acres was the location for a short-lived peace camp outside the American Embassy during President Ronald Reagan's visit in 1984. The camp was unique because an edict passed by the Garda Commissioner had the effect of allowing the Garda arrest some twenty-seven women from the camp and to hold them for the duration of Reagan's visit to Ireland. It is also of interest that Mary Robinson presented a press conference outlining the women's objections to the Reagan visit. Six and a half years later, she was to enter Áras an Uachtaráin herself as the first female President of Ireland.

Some years earlier, the murder of nurse Bridie Gargan in Phoenix Park on 22 July 1982 shocked the nation. Her killer, Malcolm McArthur, had wanted to rob a bank when his private funds began to run out and he attempted to steal Nurse Gargan's car while she sunbathed between the Main Road and the back gate of Deerfield, the US Ambassador's residence. She resisted, and McArthur attacked her with a lump hammer. Nurse Gargan died from the blows despite the best efforts of a nearby gardener to halt the attack. McArthur was subsequently arrested in the home of the attorney general of the time, Patrick Connolly, in circumstances that saw the coining of a new word, GUBU, when Taoiseach Charles Haughey TD said the events were "grotesque, unbelievable, bizarre and unprecedented". McArthur was still in prison in 2005, awaiting a decision of the parole board to release him (see also Chapter 5).

Phoenix Park was designated a national park in 1986, another milestone in its history of being a park for the people and for wildlife. In the same decade, Dublin's Millennium celebrations in 1988 saw several fireworks displays being held in the park.

In 1995, President Mary Robinson held a reception at Áras an Uachtaráin for the Heaney family when Nobel prize-winning poet Seamus Heaney returned to Ireland in triumph with his prize.

The previous year, the Irish soccer team under manager Jack Charlton was welcomed home from the World Cup by hundreds of thousands of people on the Fifteen Acres. Eight years later, the 2002 World Cup soccer team under manager Mick McCarthy also had a homecoming in Phoenix Park, this time in front of the soccer pavilions, the crowds standing on the park's own soccer pitches.

In July 1998, a row broke out over the felling of a chestnut tree cut down in controversial circumstances when cyclists competing in the Tour de France visited the park on 12 July as part of its multi-staged journey to the finishing line in Paris. Dúchas, The Heritage Service, which had taken over responsibility for the park at the time, said the tree was felled in the interests of public safety because of its proximity to the hospitality tent which had been erected in conjunction with the Tour de France and the possibility of high winds.

In 2003, athletes competing in the Special Olympics used the park for Olympics cycling events, and the defence forces ran fundraising events in the park to help the Olympic effort. Members of the Garda Síochána for their part carried the Special Olympics flame around Ireland in four torches until the runners all arrived together at Áras an Uachtaráin to be greeted at a reception by the current President Mary McAleese on 20 June. Those in attendance included President Kennedy's sister, Eunice Kennedy Shriver, founder of the Special Olympics, and granddaughter of an Irish famine emigrant herself, and her son, Tim, the president of the movement. Afterwards, the Olympic torch run left Phoenix Park for Dublin Castle and the waiting city.

Throughout the centuries, Phoenix Park has played host to the lowly and the mighty alike. Its history has not ended since it is an integral part of Dublin and the wider world and continues to play its part in the unfolding of events, as always.

2

BIG HOUSES AND
OTHER BUILDINGS

In addition to serving as functional buildings, a number of large houses in the park are also home to those living there. Áras an Uachtaráin is home to the President of Ireland and stands in its own grounds to the north of the main Chesterfield Avenue. Its main entrance is beside the roundabout at the Phoenix Column. A near neighbour is the serving United States Ambassador who lives in Deerfield House, the entrance to which is also beside the Column roundabout.

A third major building that once stood nearby housed the Papal Nuncio of the time. However, in 1978, the Nuncio moved out of the park and in the redevelopment of the site the house was discovered to be riddled with dry rot and was demolished. The older Ashtown Castle was revealed, hidden inside the larger house, and was subsequently restored as part of the present-day Phoenix Park Visitor Centre. The lines of the Papal Nuncio's house were marked out with a boxwood "maze" and now serve as a children's entertainment and facility for visitors. An upper floor of the castle was used as a chapel by the Nuncio and his staff when they were resident there.

However, long before the present uses were contemplated for the three houses, they housed the three most important government officials in Ireland. Áras an Uachtaráin, then called the Vice Regal Lodge, was home to the Viceroy or Lord Lieutenant of Ireland, who ruled as head of state in the name of the monarch of the time. What is now called Deerfield was home to the Chief Secretary, who was the equivalent to a modern Taoiseach or prime minister. The house at Ashtown Castle was home to the Under Secretary, whose equivalent would be a Tánaiste or deputy prime minister in modern times. So, within a stone's throw of one another lived the three most powerful people in the country. Indeed, so close are the dwellings that when US President John F. Kennedy visited Ireland in June 1963 he chose to walk across the park from Deerfield House, where he was staying, to Áras an Uachtaráin to meet President Eamon de Valera in his home.

Other accommodation decisions might have seen a rather different congregation of people living in the cluster of large houses at the centre of Phoenix Park, if a British request of 1942 had been acceded to by the Government. The British Ambassador to Ireland, Sir John Maffey, had sought to secure tenancy of the former Private Secretary's Lodge. The Lodge had formerly been part of the Áras grounds and was home to Winston Churchill as a small boy while his father served as Private Secretary. The Maffey proposal, coming as it did in the middle of the Second World War, was turned down for a number of reasons, one of them being that it was considered "very undesirable that . . . any branch of the Diplomatic Corps, particularly one representing a belligerent State", should be living so close to the President. Additionally, there was a fear that this close proximity to the President might be interpreted as "a form of British influence on the President", according to an Irish Diplomatic Corps memo drawn up on 15 December 1942 and held in the National Archives. In the event, a different use was found for the Lodge. Douglas Hyde, the first President of Ireland, retired in 1945 to live in the newly renamed Ratra House, where he lived for four years before his death in 1949. The house subsequently became the headquarters of the Civil Defence.

A 1942 memorandum also documented a request made by the Canadian High Commissioner to fish in the presidential lake, a request that was not only refused but also prompted the decision to terminate all fishing permits from the end of that year, according to the Office of the Secretary to the President.

Indeed, fishing in the pond must have been good because, in July 1996, an eighteen-year-old man was apprehended by President Robinson while she was walking with Nick, her husband, in the grounds. The man was fishing in a pond close to the residence and was brought to the gates by Mrs Robinson, to be handed over to security. He was later released. It was the second breach of security in a month at the house. In June, a twenty-two-year-old man, reportedly under the influence of drink, was arrested but later released. He was taken into custody by an Army officer who answered his ring at the door of Áras an Uachtaráin. The man had climbed a wall, evaded armed gardaí and passed electronic security devices in the grounds on the way to his late-night call on the President.

Curiously, if the 1942 British accommodation proposal had gone ahead, the President, the British Ambassador and the US Ambassador would all have been neighbouring park residents — as would the Taoiseach of the day, if a later plan had come to fruition.

Visitors to Phoenix Park Visitor Centre at Ashtown Castle have Charles Haughey, the former Taoiseach, to thank for access to the building. After the old papal nunciature was demolished (see below), its replacement was to have been an official Taoiseach's residence where guests would be received by the leader of the day. But when Haughey became Taoiseach he vetoed the proposal, perhaps because he did not think the public was ready for the grandeur of it all. As Haughey later told the Moriarty Tribunal, which was set up to inquire into irregular payments to politicians, his own North County Dublin home, the Gandon-designed Abbeville at Kinsealy, would do perfectly well as a Taoiseach's residence. "There was no particular need for a sparkling new armoured palace in the Phoenix Park," said Haughey. He added that he had called a halt to the proposal because Phoenix Park is "sacrosanct" and he did not think the public at the time was ready to have a specially built Taoiseach's residence, "as such".

ÁRAS AN UACHTARÁIN

Áras an Uachtaráin is the home and workplace of the President of Ireland.

The original house was built by Park Ranger Nathaniel Clements for his own use during the eighteenth century. In April 1751, at age forty-six, Clements was appointed Chief Ranger of Phoenix Park and Master of the Game. The appointment was to last for his lifetime and for the lifetimes of his three sons.

The former Vice Regal Lodge, now Áras an Uachtaráin

With the entire park to choose from, Clements picked the site of an earlier building, Newtown Lodge, to face a rolling vista of parkland, set off by the Dublin mountains in the distance. The passing life of the park on nearby Chesterfield Avenue could be seen from the house when it was completed in 1754, and provided entertainment for the residents before shrubbery and trees grew up to obscure the modern view.

The original site ran to an enclosed ninety-two acres. A stream on its northern boundary was dammed to form a small lake that became known as the Fish Pond. The grounds later came to extend to some 200 acres, though it lost acreage in the late 1990s to Dublin Zoo for its African Plains extension.

A formal tree plantation to the western side was inaugurated by the Earl of Chesterfield in 1746 and over the centuries the grounds became the ceremonial planting place of trees by visiting dignitaries. Such plantings have the double effect of, perhaps, catering to the egos of the guests and of allowing the planting of ornamental trees that might not survive the activity of the wider park.

The first house was a plain structure described by Thomas Milton in his *View of Seats* as nothing more than a neat, plain brick building with the rooms within conveniently disposed. Offices projected on either side and were joined to the house by circular sweeps. On either side of the house curved Palladian curtain walls decorated with rusticated balls led to L-shaped pavilions of three bays each, with the whole block concluding with gateways and further walls at either end enclosing offices.

Inside, the hall was top-lit at the entrance end by a window. A large saloon, with an elaborate compartmented ceiling and floral plaster, was heated by twin chimney pieces. At each end of the hall, a small vestibule led off into a further reception room. A small stairs led to the bedrooms.

In 1802, the Earl of Hardwicke ordered two new wings to be added to the Vice Regal Lodge and by 1816 a Portland stone portico of four Ionic columns had been constructed. There have been

The Portland stone portico at Áras an Uachtaráin

improvements and additions made to the house over the years, the most noteworthy being the establishment of formal gardens by Decimus Burton in the 1840s; addition of the East Wing in 1849 for the state visit of Queen Victoria; installation of mains gas supply in 1852 and electricity in 1908; and extension of the West Wing for the visit of George V in 1911.

In 1767, after a decree was issued stating that the King's representative for Ireland, the Viceroy, should reside in Ireland, the English Government bought the Lodge from the Clements family for £25,000 as an official residence. In 1778 Lord Carlisle became the first Viceroy to reside in the newly acquired building, now renamed the Vice Regal Lodge. Carlisle, whose real name was Frederick Howard, was the author of a number of poems and two tragedies, *The Father's Revenge* and *The Stepmother*, which received high praise from his contemporaries. While the first Viceroy to inhabit the building wrote poetry, it is a coincidence of history that Douglas

Hyde, the first President of Ireland to call the place his home, also wrote poetry and was a playwright. Hyde's play *Casadh an tSúgáin*, produced by the Irish Literary Theatre in October 1901, was the first play in Irish to appear on a professional stage.

As the royal representative, the Viceroy attended sessions of the Irish Parliament which were held in what is now the Bank of Ireland's premises, opposite Trinity College, on College Green in the city. The Parliament in 1800 voted itself out of existence through the Act of Union and Irish parliamentary representatives took their seats in the Westminster parliament. This had been planned and worked for by the serving Viceroy, Charles Cornwallis, a man with an international military reputation, who was appointed Viceroy in 1798, and whose legacy was discussed in Chapter 1.

Following abolition of the local parliament, Dublin's prestige diminished in the empire, and the Viceroy or Lord Lieutenant became more prominent in Irish affairs. The country was administered by the chief secretary and his staff in Dublin Castle, but the Viceroy's influence and authority could by-pass this bureaucracy when he so decided. His Phoenix Park home became the centre for fashionable society. Indeed, Viceroys were often selected for their ability to support the social responsibilities attached to the office. While it may seem quaint now, Phoenix Park was considered then to be removed from the city and the Viceroy's annual move in May from quarters in Dublin Castle to the Vice Regal Lodge marked the end of Dublin's social season. His return to the castle, once summer was spent, marked its resumption.

In its incarnations as both Vice Regal Lodge and as Áras an Uachtaráin, the house has played host to many heads of state — mostly, in the nineteenth century, British monarchs. King George IV was the first monarch to stay at the Vice Regal Lodge in 1821, followed by Queen Victoria in June 1849, on the first of her several visits to the park during her reign. She participated, with enthusiasm, in a series of receptions, dinners and visitations. Some 1,750 guests were said to have been presented to Victoria in the Vice Regal Lodge during that visit. This, while the country was reeling from mass emigration, death by starvation, and penury, in the aftermath of the potato famine of the late 1840s. More than a million people died from starvation during the famine and more than four million emigrated from a pre-famine population of some eight million people. Another armed rebellion in 1848, this time by the Young Irelanders, had been put down the year before the Queen's visit.

In fact, Victoria may have come close to being kidnapped from the Vice Regal Lodge, an event which would probably not have amused her, much. The thirty-year-old Victoria was unaware of the plot to abduct her. She was anticipating a military review in her honour the following day, on the nearby Fifteen Acres — complete with regimental bands, charging cavalry and loud huzzas in her honour. She was in residence at the Vice Regal Lodge when 200 aspiring kidnappers met on the bank of the Royal Canal, intent on action. They were armed with pistols and daggers but were strongly advised by prominent nationalist Gavan Duffy that it was not a good idea to kidnap the lady, as there were 10,000 British troops assembled in Dublin for her visit. The putative revolutionaries abandoned the plan to spirit the Queen to the mountains and glens in pursuit of Irish freedom, and went home.

In August 1861, a Californian redwood tree was planted by Queen Victoria on the second of her visits to Ireland in the garden of the Vice Regal Lodge; it can still be seen today by visitors to Áras an Uachtaráin. As the century turned, the Queen, by then an eighty-three-year-old monarch on her third visit to Ireland, stayed at the house in April 1900, for more than three weeks. The black-garbed revolutionary leader Maud Gonne staged a protest patriotic tea party opposite the Vice Regal Lodge while Victoria was in residence.

Victoria's successor, King Edward VII, and his Queen Alexandra visited Dublin in 1903 and 1907. Edward died suddenly in 1910.

His successor King George V and Queen Mary arrived in 1911 and the west wing of the Lodge was extended for their visit.

Since independence, it is the "royalty" of other countries who have provided international flavour at the Áras. In 1963, US President John F. Kennedy stayed at the Ambassador's residence when he visited Ireland. A large crush occurred when a tea party was arranged on the Áras lawns for the Kennedy visit, when the invited guests seemed to forget they were supposed to be sophisticated about the presence amongst them of the charismatic President and instead all rushed together to greet him on a warm June day in the park.

The meeting between Kennedy and Eamon de Valera was a somewhat strange meeting of two presidents. Kennedy was the US President whose grandfather had emigrated to Boston in the 1840s from County Wexford and settled in America, while de Valera was the Irish President born in Brooklyn in New York and brought to live in Ireland as an infant.

Kennedy was followed to Ireland and to Áras an Uachtaráin on formal visits by Presidents Richard Nixon (in 1970), Ronald Reagan (in 1984) and Bill Clinton (thrice, in 1995, 1998 and 2000).

Another visitor who returned several times to the park was the Emperor Akihito of Japan, who first visited as crown prince in 1953, after attending the coronation, in London, of Queen Elizabeth II. Akihito also visited the Áras in 1985, following President Patrick Hillery's state visit to Japan. Akihito planted a tree in the grounds of Áras an Uachtaráin, and returned to the house and grounds (and the tree) many years later, in 2005, by then aged seventy-two, as part of a three-day visit with the Empress Michiko. The couple stayed in Farmleigh as guests of the nation on their final visit.

More than a hundred years before Akihito's first visit, the formal gardens were designed and laid out by Decimus Burton, in the 1840s. Burton was an English landscape architect who more than anybody else was responsible for the appearance and layout of the present-day park. He designed many of the gate houses as well as the main Chesterfield Avenue, which sweeps past Áras an Uachtaráin in a broad avenue. His design of sunken fences, rather than ground-level walls, add to the visual impact of many of the park's important buildings, including Áras an Uachtaráin, where the view is unimpeded by perimeter markings. The lawns immediately to the front of the building are laid out in the form of a Celtic cross, to this day, following Burton's design.

Inside the house in the main rooms large mirrors were placed high on the walls to catch the light from the candlelight chandeliers and to reflect more illumination around the rooms. Stronger lighting became available to the residents of the big house with the installation of a mains gas supply in 1852 and of electricity in 1908. The park's roads continue to be illuminated by gas lighting, as a matter of interest, though nowadays they are switched on automatically, doing away with the necessity of the lamplighters of old, whose responsibility it was to kindle each individual light at dusk.

By 1921, independence had been achieved for most of the country and Saorstát Éireann, the Irish Free State, came into being, with Dominion status. The house in Phoenix Park then served as the official residence of the Governors General, the Crown's representatives. Irish parliamentarian and former Parnellite Tim Healy was appointed the first Governor General, and the house became his official residence. After five years in office, Healy was succeeded by James McNeill, who used the house to invite representatives of disparate groups together in an attempt at reconciliation of opposing views.

However, the office of Governor General faded from relevance in the years following the election of the first Fianna Fáil government under Eamon de Valera in 1932. Following the general election, McNeill was succeeded as Governor General by Domhnall O'Buachalla, a veteran of the 1916 Rising, who agreed to do the minimum necessary, as Governor General — to be a signatory if or when a signature was required. O'Buachalla chose not to move into the Vice Regal Lodge and never appeared formally at any public occasion, and the house lay empty for some years.

The new Constitution in 1937 heralded in the office of an elected President, an t-Uachtarán, to replace the Governor General. The presidential term of office is for seven years and a President may not serve for more than two terms. The President is also supreme commander of the Irish Defence Forces. Unlike presidents in other parts of the world, the Irish President does not have an executive or policy role. However, for a Bill to become law, it must be signed by the President, who may refer a bill to the courts to test its constitutionality before it can be enacted.

Douglas Hyde was chosen as the first President of Ireland and was inaugurated in 1938. To symbolise the new era, in 1939, Hyde planted a tree in the grounds of Áras an Uachtaráin. To date, eight Presidents have served in office (see below).

During the term of the second President, Sean T. Ó Ceallaigh (1945–59), interior renovation began, creating the now famous Francini corridor containing busts of past Presidents, along with a tiled spiral staircase. Royal portraits and a list of Ireland's Great War dead disappeared to be replaced by pictures of Pearse and Connolly. However, President Erskine Childers (1973–74) recognised the house's past royal connections once more and plaques in the grounds commemorating royal visitors were restored.

In the final decade of the twentieth century, President Mary Robinson instituted the practice of keeping a light shining in an upstairs window of the Áras as a sign of welcome home and a remembrance of the Irish diaspora around the world, which was such a factor of nineteenth- and twentieth-century Ireland. The light was placed in what was a family kitchen on the first floor of the building, where it remains lit to this day. The light may be seen from the main road of the park by passers-by, and has come to have significance beyond its local illumination.

By the early years of the twenty-first century, though not fully open to the public, some 15,000 people were visiting the house

The Francini Corridor at Áras an Uachtaráin

annually, some on official visits to meet the President, and others on the free Saturday guided tours which are open to all comers and which begin at the nearby Phoenix Park Visitor Centre. Visitors are shown the entrance hall, the President's study, the drawing room, the Council of State room, the state reception room, the dining room and the state corridor, as well as having a short tour of the gardens. The state corridor is lined with bronze busts of Irish Presidents by Irish sculptors. The presidential website, www.president.ie, also offers a virtual tour with a 360-degree vista.

While Áras an Uachtaráin is home to the President and her family, it is also a workplace where visiting dignitaries are received and foreign ambassadors present their credentials to the President. The President works in her study, and the Council of State meets in the Council of State Room when summoned by the President to advise. Newly appointed government ministers receive their seals of office from the President at Áras an Uachtaráin.

The Council of State Room

Having an official address may be swanky when you are a titled person, but the everyday effects can be somewhat difficult for ordinary families. The present incumbent, Mary McAleese, moved into the house to live in 1997 with her husband Martin and their young family. However, the youngsters soon encountered problems when ordering fast food for home delivery. When they gave the delivery address as Áras an Uachtaráin, they were at first not believed by the dispatchers (to put it mildly). In the event, the issue was resolved, but it showed that even heads of state can have delivery problems with the pizza guy!

PRESIDENTS OF IRELAND

Douglas Hyde

The first Irish President, Douglas Hyde (Dubhglas de híde) served from 25 June 1938 to 24 June 1945. Born on 17 January 1860, in County Roscommon, Hyde was a co-founder and first president of the Gaelic League, the national movement for the revival of the Irish language. A Protestant and a scholar, he was a member of Seanad Éireann, the Upper House or Senate, in the period 1925–38. On his retirement from the presidency, he took up residence in the former Lodge of the Secretary to the Lord Lieutenant to the rear of Áras an Uachtaráin where he lived out the remaining four years of his life. The house was re-named Ratra after Hyde's former home in Roscommon, a name it retains to the present day. He died on 12 July 1949.

Sean T. O'Ceallaigh

Born in 1882, Sean T. O'Ceallaigh was a founder member of Sinn Féin in 1905 and subsequently fought in the War of Independence. In 1918 he was elected to the first Dáil Éireann. Irish members elected in the 1918 British general election refused to sit at Westminster and instead met in Dublin's Mansion House as the Irish legislative assembly, Dáil Éireann. The assembly and its ministers operated as the de facto government of Ireland throughout the War of Independence. O'Ceallaigh was the Speaker of the first Dáil Éireann, 1919–21, and continued to be elected as a TD until 1945, when he became President. O'Ceallaigh served from 25 June 1945 until 1959. He died on 23 November 1966.

Eamon de Valera

Eamon de Valera was born in New York on 14 October 1882, but was brought to Ireland at two and a half years of age. He joined the Irish Volunteers on their founding in 1913. He commanded the Boland's Mills garrison in Dublin's docks area during the 1916 uprising. After the surrender, he was sentenced to death, but the sentence was commuted. De Valera was released on general amnesty in 1917. He was elected Sinn Féin MP for East Clare in 1918 and re-elected at all subsequent elections until his election as President in 1959. Following enactment of the Irish Constitution, de Valera was elected Taoiseach (Prime Minister); he served three separate terms as Taoiseach: 1937–48; 1951–54; and 1957–59. On 25 June 1959 he was inaugurated as President of Ireland and re-elected President in 1966 at the age of 83. He retired from office in June 1973 and died on 29 August 1975.

Erskine Childers

Erskine Childers was born in London on 11 December 1905. He moved to Dublin in 1931, aged twenty-six years of age, to become advertisement manager of the newly launched *Irish Press* newspaper, a paper closely associated with the Fianna Fáil party. He was elected to Dáil Éireann in 1938. He served as a minister in various governments. Childers was Tánaiste in the period 1969–73. On 25 June 1973 he was inaugurated as the fourth President of Ireland. However, he died suddenly in office on 17 November 1974 whilst attending a public function.

Cearbhall Ó Dálaigh

Cearbhall Ó Dálaigh was born on 12 February 1911, and was the first President to resign from office. A barrister by profession, he was Attorney General from 1946–48 and from 1951–53. He was Chief Justice and President of the Supreme Court 1961–73. Ó Dálaigh became President on 19 December 1974, but resigned from office on 22 October 1976 as a result of disparaging remarks made publicly about him by Paddy Donegan TD, then Minister for Defence, and of the government's subsequent unwillingness to discipline the Minister for his criticism of the President in referring a bill to the courts. Ó Dálaigh died on 21 March 1978.

Patrick J. Hillery

Patrick J. Hillery was born on 2 May 1923 in County Clare. He qualified as a medical doctor before being elected TD for Clare in 1951. He became Minister for Education in 1959. He served in a number of ministerial posts. He was inaugurated as President of

Ireland on 3 December 1976 and served until 1990, during which time he welcomed Pope John Paul II to Áras an Uachtaráin.

Mary Robinson

Mary Robinson was born on 21 May 1944 in Ballina, County Mayo. A barrister by profession, Robinson was appointed Reid Professor of Criminal Law in Trinity College Dublin when 25 years of age. A member of Seanad Éireann from 1969–89, she concurrently served as a member of Dublin City Council, 1979–83. On 3 December 1990, she was inaugurated as the seventh President of Ireland, the first female President to be elected. However, she resigned three months early from the office on 12 September 1997 to take up an appointment as United Nations High Commissioner for Human Rights.

Mary McAleese

The present incumbent, Mary McAleese, was inaugurated as the eighth President of Ireland on 11 November 1997. A barrister and former Professor of Law, McAleese was born on 27 June 1951, in Belfast, and was the first President to be born in Northern Ireland. She is married to Dr Martin McAleese. She grew up in Northern Ireland through the Troubles. Her family was adversely affected by the conflict and their home sustained damage from attackers. She has made a considerable effort in reconciliation between those of differing beliefs in Ireland. Many of opposing philosophies have found themselves seated at dinner in Áras an Uachtaráin, a house with connotations for all traditions on the island.

ASHTOWN CASTLE

Under a law passed by Henry VI in 1429, a grant of a tenner was made available to every man within the pale who within ten years built a "£10 castle" of certain minimum dimensions. Walter Foster was in 1540 leasing the lands where the castle stood for £4 a year and subletting it to two other tenants. Ashtown Castle may well have been built at this time.

The first confirmable date for the castle is in the early 1600s. It is possible it was built before then and remodelled on modern lines in the seventeenth century. The disturbed nature of the seventeenth century is reflected in the number of musket loops included in the walls to defend the castle from its owner's enemies. In any case, it is now described as a four-storey tower house.

In 1663, the Duke of Ormond bought the land, by then stretching to some 200 acres, to form part of his new park. Ashtown Castle became the residence of one of the Keepers of the Park, whose duties included walking the park and making sure nothing untoward was going on.

The Old Papal Nunciature, which was demolished in the 1970s, revealing the original Ashtown Castle

In the eighteenth century, the castle was incorporated into a larger house and in 1782 Ashtown Lodge became the residence of the Under Secretary for Ireland. The Under Secretary was also the Ranger of the Park until 1840, when the office was abolished on the death of Thomas Drummond, the last person to hold both offices.

Following independence, it was the first residence of the United States legation to Ireland until 1929 when nearby Deerfield House became the home of the US representative, which it remains to this day. From 1929, the year of the centenary celebrations of Catholic Emancipation in Ireland, it became the residence of the Papal Nuncio. A throne room was maintained in the Nunciature against the day the reigning pontiff came to visit Ireland. But in the event, the Nunciature closed in 1978, just a year before Pope John Paul II visited the park to celebrate mass for more than a million people.

It was around this time that the serving Taoiseach Charles Haughey TD opted to live in grandeur in his own house in Kinsealy rather than in a purpose-built Taoiseach's residence, and it was decided that a visitors' centre would be developed on the site instead. Restoration began in autumn 1989. The castle had been heavily altered in the eighteenth and nineteenth centuries with the insertion of Georgian windows, new floors and roof. Today, it is maintained as a museum to be visited by twenty-first-century visitors who nonetheless must make their way from floor to floor by way of a narrow winding stone staircase, just as the original occupants had to do in centuries past. However, they are unlikely to meet armed defenders pouring scorn — and more — down upon their heads as they ascend.

A restaurant, the Fionn Uisce, has been developed beside the restored castle and is managed by lessees to a high but affordable standard. Across the cobbled courtyard a Visitor Centre has been developed which features on the ground floor an audio-visual display of the park and its history, an exhibition area, and the papal chair from the 1979 papal visit to the park. Upstairs, a display is laid out covering nature in the park and highlighting some of the major

Ashtown Castle shortly after restoration

events in park life. There is a separate area dedicated to explaining nature for younger visitors.

It is said that secret tunnels connected the three houses of power at some stage to allow for access and, more importantly, for egress in a hurry if matters took a turn for the worse at any time. If they were there, they are not accessible nowadays. With the volume of motor cars passing through the park reaching 30,000 a day, and local politicians calling for commuter buses to be allowed down the main road, if the tunnels are ever found they might be pressed into service as pedestrian underpasses for crossing Chesterfield Avenue!

DEERFIELD HOUSE, THE AMERICAN AMBASSADOR'S RESIDENCE

In 1772, Sir John Blaquiere was named Bailiff of Phoenix Park, in addition to his duties as the then Chief Secretary. As bailiff he received a four-roomed cottage at what is now Deerfield, which he extended into a Georgian house on sixty acres. However, Blaquiere was challenged in a Dublin court following his annexation of some thirty acres of the park for his new residence. The court found in his favour. The house was finished in 1776 and the government bought it as an official residence for the Chief Secretary of Ireland for £7,000 in 1782.

Of passing interest is the tenure of W.H. Smith who, in 1886, took the job of Chief Secretary and lasted just four days before the government of the day resigned. Smith was a bookseller by trade and his appointment to Ireland caused him to turn over his Dublin branch to Charles Eason, his manager of some years. Both W.H. Smith and the Eason chains of booksellers and stationers continue to trade widely and successfully to this day.

The house remained as official residence of the Chief Secretary until 1922 when the last holder, Sir Harman Greenwood, left office, after which it was left idle for some years.

On 27 February 1927, the US envoy to the Irish Free State, Texan Frederick A. Sterling, presented his credentials and opened a ministerial legation in Dublin. The property was rented from the Board of Works in 1929 and until 1948 housed both the residence and the chancellery. In 1949 the post of minister was changed to an ambassadorial post and in that year a 999-year lease was signed with the OPW and the US took over the maintenance of the property.

More recently, a diary of the house was written by Elizabeth Shannon, wife of former US Ambassador Bill Shannon. The Shannons lived at the house from July 1977 to June 1981, by which time the house had been renamed Deerfield.

Extensive renovations to the house and property were made by the US Government in 1952. The property now consists of sixty-two acres of lawn, orchards and gardens on which are located the Ambassador's residence, three cottages and a gate lodge. The lower ground floor includes a ballroom, reception and dining room, library, office, kitchens, pantry, staff room and laundry. Six suites, consisting of bedroom, bathroom and dressing room, plus a sitting room, are located on the upper floor. The ground floor's two drawing rooms and ballroom interconnect to make a large single space when desired.

The house and grounds are private and enjoy a high level of security. However, visits of appropriate groups are accommodated throughout the year and the Fourth of July Independence Day celebrations usually feature an open-air barbecue and party, depending on who is currently resident in the park.

An impressive set of entrance gates now greets official visitors to the house. Mature trees and shrubbery obscure the view of the main house from the entrance and from Chesterfield Avenue. However, the house can be seen quite clearly from the Fifteen Acres where obstructions have been cleared to allow its residents a clear view of the rolling grassland and the mountains in the distance.

Those looking in will stand in the area where in 1963 the helicopter of President Kennedy landed to take him on his travels around Ireland. In those long-ago days of Camelot, local children were allowed into the waiting helicopter, which rose a few feet off the ground to give the youngsters the thrill of their lives. They disembarked when the relaxed President of the United States came out through a wicket gate to fly away in the helicopter, but not without having first posed for local snaps.

Accompanying her brother on that visit was a young Jean Kennedy-Smith who would return to Deerfield in her own right as US Ambassador to Ireland in the 1990s. The house was host to a society Kennedy wedding on 19 August 1995 when Kym Jean Kennedy-Smith, the ambassador's daughter, married Ashtown man, Alfie Tucker, in University Church and the reception was held on a warm autumn day in Deerfield House. The couple arrived from their wedding in Dublin in a horse-drawn carriage, recalling earlier days in the park.

In vivid contrast to the equanimity of horse carriages, US President Bill Clinton and his wife Hilary in September 1998 made a dramatic night-time helicopter landing at the papal cross during a visit related to the peace process. Three Chinook troop carriers and two Nighthawk aircraft touched down beside the papal cross, delivering the large entourage. The Clintons were welcomed by Taoiseach Bertie Ahern and US Ambassador Kennedy-Smith before they decamped to the waiting Deerfield House for the night.

FARMLEIGH

Artillery units of the Irish army fired round after round at Farmleigh house and grounds on the western perimeter of Phoenix Park in the late summer of 2001. As they fired, smoke drifted across the seventy-eight acres of gardens and rolling lawns while both native and visitor alike cheered the booming of the guns.

No damage was caused, however, as the artillery was engaged in firing blank rounds to supply the cannon effect for Tchaikovsky's *1812 Overture*. The overture was performed by RTÉ's Symphony Orchestra on 28 July after An Taoiseach Bertie Ahern TD, in the company of 8,000 invited guests, conducted the opening ceremony of the nineteenth-century house and grounds as the State's first official guesthouse.

Both the *Overture* and Farmleigh itself date from the 1880s, the decade coincidentally in which Guinness shares were first floated on the stock exchange, by Farmleigh's then owner, Edward Cecil Guinness. Originally a small Georgian house built in the late eighteenth century, Farmleigh was purchased by Edward Cecil Guinness on his marriage to his cousin, Adelaide Guinness, in

Farmleigh

1873. Edward was a great-grandson of Arthur Guinness, founder of the brewery that carried his name. Edward Cecil became the first Earl of Iveagh in 1919.

Irish architect James Franklin Fuller designed the extension of the house to the west, refurbishment of the existing house, and addition of a third storey in 1881–84. By 1896, the ballroom wing was added. A new conservatory was added in a space adjoining the ballroom in 1901, where it currently stands, in its refurbished manifestation.

Outside the main doors and underneath the portico the ground is inset with wooden blocks to deaden the sound of iron-rimmed wheels on horse-drawn carriages arriving at the house. A useful addition in its day, the blocks nowadays have been known to trap the shoe heels of the unwary.

Farmleigh remained in the ownership of the Guinness family through the remainder of the nineteenth century and throughout the twentieth, until it was placed on the market as the twenty-first century dawned.

An offer to sell Farmleigh House at IR£15 million (€19.05 million) was declined by the Irish government in 1998. But when a year later the Office of Public Works (OPW) did purchase the house and grounds from the Guinness family, the market price had risen to IR£23 million (€29.20 million) for the nineteenth-century estate. However, much-needed renovation, refurbishment, upgrading and modern security brought the bill to IR£41 million (€52 million), which was a bargain, according to Martin Cullen TD, Junior Minister for the Environment, who was in charge of the purchase and renovation.

Under OPW supervision some 600 workers undertook the extensive conservation work and refurbishment to turn Farmleigh into a guesthouse fit for the lodging of kings, plenipotentiaries, premiers, presidents and princes.

On initial examination, OPW surveyors discovered dry rot in the basement, disintegrating iron nails holding slates on the roof, dangerous glass fittings in the conservatory, not to mention plumbing problems. Asbestos was found in some parts of the building. And the conservatory was placed out of bounds, such was the frequency of glass dropping from a height to the ground below from the ironwork rotted in the roof.

Many of the tradesmen's skills needed to restore the house had been lost and the OPW spent time and effort in researching methods and training craftsmen to replicate the original work. The house had to be rewired, restored, double-glazed and re-plastered in places. According to Minister Cullen, "The objective was to retain as much as possible of the rich architectural heritage of Farmleigh, while adapting its function to modern occasions."

The OPW appointed project manager Mary Heffernan as its first General Manager at Farmleigh in 2001 when the house opened for business. Ms Heffernan had been at Farmleigh since the OPW took possession on 15 December 1999 and had a major say in the selection of furnishing, fabrics and finishes.

Farmleigh is not actually in Phoenix Park, but is situated between Phoenix Park and Castleknock Road. Its main entrance is off the park itself, beside White's Gate near to the Ordnance Survey, and was the only private residence to have such a facility from the public park. Another entrance opens on the far side of the property onto Castleknock Road.

The property includes the large house with examples of Georgian/Victorian architecture: a sunken garden, a walled garden, a prominent clock tower and a lake. Farmleigh House covers 3,716 square metres over four floors. The top floor has two bedrooms and three self-contained suites, for heads of state and other important guests. In the bathrooms, free-standing circular glass showers are complemented by centrally located bath tubs. The suites are named the Iveagh, the Collins and the de Valera suites. All are finished with quality Irish materials and design, and furnished with appropriate furniture, including four-poster beds. Much of the contemporary furniture used in the house was already in the possession of the OPW and was held in storage. The de Valera suite, for instance, features the "de Valera love seat", a two-seater couch where two people can relax, sitting facing one another, which is known to have belonged to the de Valera family. However, many of the modern pieces were commissioned especially for the building.

The first floor has nine rooms furnished in a traditional fabric-walled Edwardian/Victorian style. The accommodation is to five-star hotel standard and is provided for supporting members of a delegation.

A high-ceilinged narrow corridor runs west to east through the centre of the house, linking the dining room, the entrance hall and the stairway to the upper floors. Chandeliers in the corridor are scaled-down replicas of Waterford Glass chandeliers which were presented, in 1965, by the Iveaghs to Westminster Abbey on its 900th anniversary.

The ground floor, many of whose walls are covered with original tapestries and linen, contains the dining room, library, drawing rooms, the ballroom, the Nobel Room and refurbished conservatory. The dining room is lined with seventeenth-century

Italian embroidered silk panels and dressed with new drapes hand-stitched by a seventy-two-year-old Dublin seamstress for the opening of the house.

The present-day library was originally two separate rooms, but the dividing wall was removed in 1884 and the ceiling heightened to allow for an upper gallery to be accommodated. The room is panelled in Austrian oak which yields a warming intimate atmosphere. Benjamin Guinness, Third Earl of Iveagh (1937–92), acquired a unique collection of rare books, manuscripts and first editions, including one of Jonathan Swift's *Gulliver's Travels*, many of which are on loan from the family and remain in the library.

Next door is the 1820s-style Nobel Room. The window is set above a fireplace to create a living landscape painting of the garden beyond. When the outside fountain is activated, occupants of the room can see fire and water at the same time. The chimney flue is diverted and incorporated into the wall of the room. Apart from the elements, the room celebrates the achievements of the four Irish Nobel Laureates for literature: W.B. Yeats, George Bernard Shaw, Samuel Beckett and Seamus Heaney. James Joyce, who was not a Nobel Laureate, is included for good measure. A poem written by Seamus Heaney on the occasion of the 2004 May Day gathering of the heads of state at Farmleigh is on display (see Chapter 6).

The ballroom is the largest room in the house, measuring 23.32 metres in length by 7.85 metres in width, and was built in the Edwardian era when people thought it proper to have a private ballroom within the home, as you do. The wood for the oak floor may or may not have come from disused barrels at the brewery, but its provenance has never been confirmed. The floor was reconstructed from the basement below and repaired, cleaned and sanded to its present sparkling condition.

In the conservatory, the dangerous glass and holding framework was replaced to provide a light-filled glassed-over space off the ballroom. Horticulturalist Liz Morgan sourced plants popular a century earlier to re-stock the conservatory for modern times. The

The conservatory at Farmleigh

airy white space is a contrast to the dark masculine feel of the restored billiards room on a landing between floors.

Farmleigh operates on two levels. There is the house and its tradition and restoration, and there is the concomitant use as a modern conference and meeting facility. It is at basement level that the modern Farmleigh is designed to play its part in the affairs of the nation. A study on the ground floor hides a false door built into a corner bookcase. An escape route was developed in the 1970s by Benjamin Guinness, third Earl of Iveagh, when kidnapping for ransom by criminal gangs and paramilitaries was at its height. Steps lead down to a vault where steel doors would seal in the occupants until rescue arrived. The vault was provided with a phone link to the outside.

The lower exit of the vault leads out to a corridor along which former staff quarters have been re-designed as conference rooms for when proximity talks took place during Northern peace talks. On this lower ground floor, or the old serving quarters, delegates meet in the high-ceilinged former kitchen. The space is two storeys high under a glass roof, and contains two old cooking ranges and other kitchen equipment. A twenty-foot pitch pine table was commissioned specially for the room, and its twenty-two oak chairs are upholstered in hide.

"I insisted that the room retain the name of The Kitchen so that a lot of work will be done in it by delegates," said Minister Cullen. The Kitchen is used by Irish government ministers when the cabinet meets in Farmleigh. The house is also used for meetings of the North-South Council of Ministers.

Elsewhere, a modern kitchen has been built, while the suites upstairs contain domestic-sized kitchens for self-contained catering. This basement level also contains meeting rooms, offices and service areas for staff and visitors. There are display and exhibition areas including health and fitness facilities, and a two-lane fitness swimming pool.

Outside, there is a lake, walled gardens, parkland, and domesticated donkeys whose pasture doubles as a helicopter landing pad. Nearby, in a secure area, is a €1.27 million security room linked to an outside satellite communications farm which can broadcast directly to as far away as China, if needs be. More than €2.5 million was spent on security to close down the walled estate in an emergency and against intrusion. Banks of monitors relay images from around the house and the estate to the underground security centre.

First guests of the nation at Farmleigh were the Chinese Premier Zhu Rongji, who arrived on 3 September 2001 with his entourage (and accompanying demonstrators). Razor wire was stretched around the walls to secure the estate during the visit.

A much larger closedown was to come on 1 May 2004 when ten new states were admitted to the EU and the Heads of State of all twenty-five EU countries gathered at Farmleigh. Security forces extended their area of enforcement into Phoenix Park and access to the park was restricted during the visits.

Other distinguished visitors who have stayed at Farmleigh include the Prime Minister of Ethiopia, and the King and Queen of Malaysia. Japan's royal Emperor Akihito and his Empress Michiko, both published poets, stayed at Farmleigh in May 2005.

In the grounds, the landmark clock tower rises to some thirty-seven metres in height. Erected in 1880, the view from its balcony stretches on a clear day from Malahide to the north, Dun Laoghaire and Dublin mountains to the south, and Maynooth to the west. The

An autumn view of Farmleigh clock tower

tower is said to have been erected by the engineering department of Guinness Brewery. The walls are 1.22 metres thick at ground level, reducing to 0.76 metres at top.

Two clock dials, 3.35 metres in diameter, feature on the east and west faces of the tower below the balcony. They are cast in iron, painted and gilded, and the hands are copper. The clock mechanism has three sections: the time, strike and chime sections. The chime section controls five hammers to strike four bells on the quarter hour to play the Westminster chime. The strike section controls one hammer to strike the largest of the five bells on the hour. The clock remains in perfect working order and, until recently, was wound every day by hand. The weights are now raised electrically but there has been no alteration to the clock itself.

The tower contains an 8,183-litre water tank at balcony level and once provided a private water supply for the estate. A weir was constructed on the Liffey at the Strawberry Beds near the Wren's Nest pub, and a mile-long millrace channelled water to turn a turbine, which pumped water to the tower and generated electricity for the house. The lines were taken across the Liffey on an iron bridge specially erected for the task. The bridge was also used by those staff at Farmleigh who lived on the south side of the river as a short cut on their way to the house. The bridge is in a decrepit condition today but continues to span the river and the road near the Angler's Rest pub. The bridge and its preservation are the responsibility of Fingal County Council.

Elsewhere in the grounds, a focal point is the lawn at the back of the house, which rises gently up to a large circular fountain with a single high water jet — the same fountain that is framed in the window of the Nobel Room. The fountain and lawn are enclosed by mature copper, beech and lime trees. On the western side of the lawn are the dairy and the cherry walk, which leads to the sunken garden. The walled garden for its part covers about four acres and is sloped towards the south. A stone temple was created as another focal point of the garden by Benjamin and Miranda Guinness in 1971.

Farmleigh serves both as a state guesthouse and a heritage area where public access is allowed at designated times when affairs of State are not in progress.

Even though the house belongs to the State, local planning laws require that Fingal County Council be the planning authority for certain events. Dublin City Council is the planning authority for Phoenix Park generally. Planning permission is approved by Fingal for public events for up to 8,000 guests on days between June and September. Events for up to 1,000 people may be held between April and October, and recreational activities on any day between June and September for not more than 500 people is permitted.

The OPW presents a public access programme, which provides opportunity to enjoy the Farmleigh house and grounds. The programme includes cultural events covering music, gardens, food, literature and art and design. A special programme is also presented at Easter and Christmas. All events are presented to the public free of charge. An art gallery opened in 2005 to the public from Thursdays to Sundays. A popular Farmers' Market, including food talks and appearances by celebrity chefs, takes place in the old stableyard, in season.

Free tours of the house and grounds are available on designated weekends. More than 10,000 visitors took up the offer of a free tour at weekends in the month following the official opening. Visitors are restricted to the grounds and the ground floor of the house; but organised tours may apply for permission to visit the upper parts of the house, as appropriate.

A tearoom/restaurant operates in an old boathouse beside the lake, and during the midwinter the house and grounds are decorated in traditional Christmas style. Music recitals and choirs entertain visitors to the house with seasonal and traditional fare. For many, a trip to Farmleigh is becoming a Christmas tradition of its own.

Farmleigh is accessed through Phoenix Park and off the White's Gate Road. The house is a fifteen-minute walk from Castleknock gate for those arriving by public transport. There is ample car parking on site. Special interest groups can arrange tours of the gardens, the silver exhibition and the art collection or of the unique Guinness library by appointment. The Motorhouse Café is situated in the courtyard and provides light refreshments which can be enjoyed in the café or in the pleasure grounds. Details of events, promotions and opening times may be found on the website, www.farmleigh.ie.

St Mary's Hospital

The 327-bed St Mary's Hospital provides a wide range of services for the elderly population resident on the north side of Dublin. St Mary's was built in 1765 and, as the Royal Hibernian Academy, provided for the education and care of children of British Army personnel until 1924. The children were either orphans of soldiers or their fathers were posted overseas. A 1765 census showed there to be some 1,400 children in Dublin whose soldier fathers were either dead or serving abroad. Some had mothers still alive, some were from families grown too large for the parents to cope and were placed in care. Some remained in the Academy until they eventually left as apprentices, or as recruits to the army or into domestic service. Preference was given to boys over girls and eventually girls were removed to the Drummond School in Chapelizod. Training was provided within the Academy for future life and to a great extent the institution was self-sufficient. Children between the ages of seven and twelve years of age were accepted into the Academy — provided they were sound of mind and body. Those who developed fits after they were admitted were discharged from the Academy, under the regulations.

The Lord Lieutenant attended services in the Academy's chapel when he was in residence in the Vice Regal Lodge. Funds were originally raised to preserve the children from popery, beggary and idleness, and to train them to be useful Protestant subjects. However, following Catholic Emancipation in 1829, the situation changed and, in 1847, a Catholic chaplain was appointed to the Academy. A Catholic chapel was opened in 1848 and Catholic teachers were admitted to staff in 1869.

The hospital was returned to the Free State when the Hibernian Academy moved to England after Irish Independence was achieved and was subsequently operated by the Irish Army as a hospital before being developed as a TB hospital and then into its modern use.

The next-door Cara Cheshire House was built in 1974 as the first purpose-built Cheshire Home in Ireland. Cara accommodates thirty-two adult disabled service users and provides respite services. Service users contribute to the day-to-day running of the house and, where possible, integrate with the local community.

ORDNANCE SURVEY

Almost within sight of the Cheshire Home, the headquarters of Ordnance Survey Ireland are in Mountjoy House, in buildings that were originally the residence of Luke Gardiner, before housing the mounted escort to the Lord Lieutenant resident nearby in the Vice Regal Lodge (now Áras an Uachtaráin).

The house was originally built in 1728. Gardiner was appointed Keeper of the Castleknock Walk in 1778, and occupied the house. In Gardiner's time, the Lodge over the years was the scene of theatrical productions of Shakespearean plays, events which were attended by the Lord Lieutenant and others of the ruling classes of the time. Gardiner was later to become Lord Mountjoy.

The Ordnance Survey took up residence in the park in 1824, some few years after the Napoleonic Wars and the prospect of a French invasion in Ireland had ended. George IV's Royal Warrant said it would be "advantageous to Our Service to raise an additional

Company of Royal Sappers and Miners to be employed in the operations of the Survey in Ireland". The new operation, under the command of Major W. Reid, was established in Mountjoy House by Lt. Col. Thomas Colby. Its British counterpart was used to map those parts of England that French invaders might have used during the Anglo-French hostilities. In Ireland, the task was to measure, survey and map the whole of Ireland. The survey was used to update land valuations for taxation purposes. A fire-proof store was built at Mountjoy in 1827 to house the fair plans and documents relating to the survey. However, in the 1990s, much of the documentation was removed from Phoenix Park to the National Archives for safekeeping.

By 1846, the entire island had been surveyed at a scale of six inches to one mile. Interestingly, Ireland was the first country in the world to be entirely mapped on such a detailed scale.

Following the establishment of Saorstát Éireann in 1922, the British Ordnance Survey, which had been responsible for both islands, was divided into three bodies. In Ireland, the Ordnance Survey of Northern Ireland was established on 1 January 1922 and the Ordnance Survey based in Phoenix Park took responsibility on 1 April 1922 for the survey requirements of the rest of Ireland.

Irish Ordnance Survey maps were used during the Second World War by the German High Command, who drew up maps of landing beaches in Wexford for possible invasion of Ireland. While they were planning to invade, creosote-soaked wooden sleepers were being driven into the ground of Fifteen Acres by the Irish army to prevent enemy forces from landing there. Rolls of barbed wire were stretched above Chesterfield Avenue for the same purpose.

The Ordnance Survey Company was dis-established on 1 November 1998, in accordance with the re-organisation of the Defence Forces. Personnel of the former Ordnance Survey Company were deployed to the Logistics Battalion, 2nd Eastern Brigade, pending phasing out of military involvement with Ordnance Survey Ireland. Of forty non-commissioned personnel serving in the Ordnance Survey Company, twenty-eight applied to the Civil Service Commission for appointment to Ordnance Survey Ireland. The remaining two officers and twelve non-commissioned personnel were redeployed within the Defence Forces. On 4 March 2002, Ordnance Survey Ireland was vested as a state body.

The OSI originates all of the maps used in Ireland today. Mountjoy House and the surrounding buildings still serve as the headquarters of Ordnance Survey Ireland, and families of survey workers live in the houses there. However, under recent decentralisation plans the Ordnance Survey office was scheduled for transfer to Dungarvan, County Waterford, though there is no indication as to when, or indeed if, this will actually happen.

GATES, LODGES AND OTHER BUILDINGS

While Phoenix Park is best known for its big houses, its rolling acres and its mix of recreational uses, it also contains a selection of architecturally interesting smaller buildings and lodges. There are some thirty-eight lodges with living accommodation situated within Phoenix Park and no two dwellings are of the same design.

The wall is itself designated as a protected structure and stretches the entire way around the present-day park. It is eleven kilometres long and three metres high. The present-day wall follows on from the wall constructed by Sir John Temple, after the earlier wall built by a contractor called Dodson had proved to have been built with poor material and shoddy workmanship and consistently fell down (see Chapter 1).

The outside face of the wall is the park's boundary. Consequently, any encroachment on the wall can be challenged by park management. Encroachment includes erecting sheds or other structures against the outside wall. Posting notices on the wall is not allowed, and using the wall for stays for poles or aerials,

Sketch by Pat Liddy of the main gates at Parkgate Street

the erection of tents against the wall, and the dumping of refuse without authority are all forbidden.

Each of the vehicular gates into Phoenix Park has a gatekeeper's lodge as part of the entrance cluster. At one time, all entrances had an accompanying constable's hut that was manned during the opening hours of the gates. The constables were there to prevent anything of value being spirited out of the park. They also served to prevent entry to banned vehicles under the terms of the 1925 Act which governs the park. Commercial vehicles require a permit to enter, and the permit specifies which gates may be used for the purpose of the licensee's business in the park.

The Commissioners of Public Works established a modern park ranger unit in 1989 to deal with the enforcement of the bylaws and regulations. Rangers patrol the park in pairs in jeeps, while their solitary predecessors used the trusty bicycle for generations. Discussion on the changes led to some picketing by employees and the park witnessed its rangers standing outside the entrance gates on strike pickets. With the issues resolved, the change did not affect the tenancies of employees resident in the park who are allocated park homes as part of their employment.

Employees living in the lodges are subject to regulations first promulgated in 1919. They preclude the keeping of goats, pigs or cattle by the ranger at the lodge. Poultry keeping is restricted to areas approved by park management. In addition, the regulations forbid male children over the age of eighteen and females over the age of twenty-one from residing in the lodge without specific permission. Permission has to be applied for annually on 1 January.

On the right of the main entrance at Parkgate Street is a single-storey gatekeeper's house that was built in 1811. What is not visible is the old public gallows for the county that used to stand in this area. It was moved in 1646 to a new location at Kilmainham to make room for building at the main park gates in the early days of the development of Phoenix Park as a royal deer park.

The gatekeeper's lodge and another now-ruined building on the opposite side of Chesterfield Avenue were part of an old Dublin Metropolitan Police barracks built strategically at the entrance to the park and at the start of the city's quays with clear access for constabulary in either direction.

Within the People's Flower Gardens there is a lodge built for the Gardens' keeper. *Dignam's Dublin Guide* of 1891 said that a residence "like a Swiss chalet" was erected over the lake for the head gardener.

Beside the People's Gardens the old infirmary stands above a valley where convalescent soldiers used to take their exercise. A red lodge stands in the valley and is fenced off as part of the army headquarters enclosure.

The view from the Gardens includes the entrance to Dublin Zoo which came into being in 1830. A number of buildings are situated inside the grounds of the zoo that are of interest, and these are discussed in Chapter 9.

The Islandbridge lodge and gates are part of a number of lodges designed or redesigned by Burton in the period between 1830 and 1845. A viewing spot opposite the gate was used by artists to paint views of the Liffey as it flows towards the city. The famous Malton images were painted from here in the late eighteenth and early nineteenth centuries (an example can be seen on page 8). The Glacis Lodge stands at the foot of the slope leading up to the Magazine Fort, which houses several more lodges and gatehouses.

As one travels along the corkscrew Military Road and past the disused magazine on St Thomas' Hill with the River Liffey flowing below on the way to the next Burton-designed gates at Chapelizod, one comes to the Timekeeper's Lodge and the Deer Lodge, also designed by Burton in 1849. The Timekeeper's or Fort Lodge was the home of the Assistant Park Superintendent. While in modern times the Deer Lodge is used to house park constables and their families, the Lodge was home to the Deerkeeper, who stabled his

Chapelizod Gates

horse there and who rode out to inspect the deer. As a mark of his authority, this Ranger wore stripes on his jacket and carried a rifle loaded with ball shot in a scabbard on the horse.

At nearby Chapelizod, the gates and lodge were designed by Burton to replace an older entrance at nearby Park Lane. The vehicular entrance was moved so that people entering the park could see the Hibernian Academy, now part of St Mary's Hospital, stretching across the ridge in front of them. The park wall was extended across Park Lane to close off the earlier entrance and a turnstile was inserted in the wall for access.

A signposted path now leads from this stile to the top of Knockmary Hill where an ancient cromlech is to be found. The Bronze-Age burial cist dates from around 2500 BC and was discovered in 1838 when landscaping work was being carried out under Burton's design. Two male skeletons discovered in the cist were removed to the National Museum of Ireland.

The cromlech is located beside the Park Ranger's house on Knockmary Hill, which is currently occupied by Ranger Jim Manning and his family. Three generations of the Manning family have been associated with service in the park and Áras an Uachtaráin since

Knockmaroon Gates and Lodge

Some of the lodges and cottages in Phoenix Park, including Islandbridge Gate and Lodge . . .

. . . The Deerkeeper's Lodge . . .

. . . The Rose Cottage . . .

*. . . Castleknock
Gate Lodge . . .*

*. . . The Bailiff's
Lodge . . .*

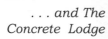

*. . . and The
Concrete Lodge*

the nineteenth century. From the hill can be seen the park wall continuing its way around the park perimeter.

Knockmaroon Gates, also designed by Burton, were once exit points for leisure drives from the city through Phoenix Park to the rural Strawberry Beds. One of the most impressive entrances to the park, the gate complex was laid out in the 1840s at a cost of £1,050. It features two sets of vehicular entrances. However, the entrance leading directly to Furry Glen has been closed for many years as the glen area was developed as a wilderness protection area.

A nearby circular interpretative centre for the wilderness area is no longer in use and interpretation is now provided at Ashtown Castle Visitor Centre, some distance away. On the way to the next entrance at White's Gate can be seen the hexagonal Rose Cottage near the Ordnance Survey office, built in the early part of the nineteenth century and currently occupied by the park deerkeeper as a home.

The vehicular entrance at White's Gate was closed in the 1990s in an attempt to introduce traffic control to the western side of the park. A pedestrian gate allows for walkers to pass through. Here too is a gatekeeper's lodge, as there is at nearby Castleknock and Ashtown Gates.

However, at Ashtown a pair of buildings protect the gates. Ashtown Gate Lodge is the main lodge but there is also Bessborough Lodge East which, along with the facing Bessborough Lodge West, formed Bessborough police barracks in times past. The former barracks now provides housing for park staff. Designed by Burton as a barracks and accommodation for police, it was completed in 1848. Burton also designed Ashtown Gate Lodge and Castleknock Gate. The nearby Bailiff's Lodge, situated within the Whitefields park administration and operations depot, was designed by Jacob Owen in 1832 and is now home to the Park Superintendent.

Further along the Back Road skirting the northern perimeter of the park road lies Phoenix Park School and beside it the Swiss cottage design of the Concrete Lodge, so called because mass concrete was

Phoenix Park School

used in its construction. In 1847, the Commissioners of Woods and Forests constructed the Phoenix Park School and residence to provide for the education of the children of its employees. The OPW took over management of the school and continued to direct its services until 1923. By 1927, the school, now renamed St Joseph's, had 120 pupils on its roll, providing for the education of children in the surrounding Cabra, Castleknock and Navan Road areas. However, in the 1960s a number of schools were established in the general area, resulting in the closure of the park school. The OPW permitted the re-opening of the school in 1975 as a special school for pupils aged between five and eleven years with emotional and behavioural difficulties from a broad catchment area. In 2005, tenders were sought for a new school building to meet the needs of the pupils and staff. The tender contract was for refurbishment of the 155-square-metre school, a protected structure, and construction of a 435-square-metre single-storey extension to the school. The school also continues to be used as a polling station during elections by park residents and by the presidential household.

The nearby Cabra Gate on Blackhorse Avenue is another of the nine vehicular access points to the park. Proposals in the 1830s to relocate the lodge and entrance, combined with partial closure of the back road, were not proceeded with.

An imposing two-storey building at the Garda Depot stands behind a fence now shielding it from the road. It is now a Garda Officers' Club. The building dates from 1863 and is the design of Benjamin Woodward, whose work in Ireland also includes the museum building in Trinity College Dublin and the original Kildare Street Club.

The North Circular Road entrance to Phoenix Park is almost as busy a thoroughfare as are the main gates at Parkgate Street and, again, a gatekeeper's lodge watches over the entrance. The North Circular Road Gate is of interest to football fans since — as recalled in a plaque at the gate — it was the secure holding place in the 1890s for goalposts belonging to the young Bohemians Football Club, who played their matches on the Nine Acres near the polo grounds but who removed the goalposts to the lodge for safekeeping after each game.

The gate lodge is just one of the dwellings in Phoenix Park with its own history and uniqueness, together making up the tapestry of life and structure that is Phoenix Park.

3

Monuments and Memorials

A number of memorials, monuments and public sculptures stand in corners of the park to commemorate people who have gone before or to provide a focus for different areas of the park. Some are so large they dominate the landscape, like the Wellington Monument, standing at sixty-three metres in height, which would have been even higher if the publicly subscribed funding had not run out. Some are not so large, like the bust of the nineteen-year-old Sean Heuston in the People's Flower Gardens, which faces the gate on Fountain Road near Gough roundabout, but they reflect events of momentous importance on the island of Ireland.

Some are gone, but their space remains and decisions have yet to be made on a new use for the vacated areas. A statue of Lord Gough that used to dominate the first crossroads encountered in the park on the way in from Dublin city was taken down, in the 1950s, after several explosives assaults on it by nationalists.

Further up Chesterfield Avenue, the Phoenix Column stands in the middle of a roundabout in memory of Lord Chesterfield, the Viceroy who in 1745 threw open the gates of the King's deer park to the people. While the Phoenix Column once dominated the centre of the park, it now yields height and visual impact to the huge cross erected at the time of the 1979 visit to the park of Pope John Paul II.

On the other side of the Phoenix Column and inside the grounds of Áras an Uachtaráin, at the end of the Queen's Walk, stands the pietà donated by the Italian government to the Irish people after the Second World War, for food assistance rendered to the Italian people, following the end of hostilities.

Across the Fifteen Acres from the cross on the road to Chapelizod there is a memorial, in St Mary's Hospital, to those men who had lived in the care of the Hibernian Academy as young boys and who died on active service in British wars, as adults.

GOUGH

A four-year-old Winston Churchill, living in 1878 in the Private Secretary's Lodge behind the Vice Regal Lodge, witnessed his grandfather John Winston Spencer-Churchill, the seventh Duke of Marlborough and Viceroy, talking loudly to the crowd gathered for the unveiling of the Lord Gough equestrian statue on Chesterfield Avenue. Churchill wrote later that he saw the Duke amongst a great black crowd, with scarlet soldiers on horseback milling about at the unveiling of the statue.

The bronze equestrian statue by John Henry Foley, standing as it did at an important crossroads, became a focal point for directions and guides, much as the Papal Cross has become in recent times. Nonetheless, much like his near neighbour, Wellington, the statue of Lord Gough, the great warrior of India, was intended for a city street location — the west side of O'Connell Bridge — but the Dublin Corporation of the time refused the request to place it there.

In the second half of the twentieth century, having survived the dropping of a bomb at the nearby Dog Pond by a German aircraft in 1942, the Gough statue was attacked with explosives by nationalists set on removing all vestiges of British rule, and on 23 July 1957 it was removed by park management from its location and sold off. An earlier attack had seen the statue's head being cut

The Gough Memorial, as it once stood

off and dumped into the River Liffey, from where it was recovered, after some time, and replaced.

In 1990, Albert Reynolds TD, the then Minister for Finance, told the Dáil that the Gough statue had been relocated in England by 1986. "It was formerly owned by the State. It was sold on the grounds that it was unlikely to be re-erected in a public place in Ireland," he said.

The official park Christmas tree is currently erected on the spot each year to welcome visitors to the park, and there is some talk of restoring a permanent feature to the roundabout to serve much the same distinctive purpose as the Phoenix Column further up Chesterfield Avenue currently serves.

WELLINGTON

Designed by the architect Sir Robert Smirke to commemorate the victories of the Iron Duke — Arthur Wellesley, Duke of Wellington — the memorial was the tallest obelisk in Europe when built. It is sixty-three metres tall and was intended to be 4.5 metres taller but failed to achieve this height for a shortage of funds.

Dublin-born Arthur Wellesley was appointed Chief Secretary for Ireland in 1806 and served until 1809, having already been an Irish MP in the now defunct parliament. Later, as the Duke of Wellington, he commanded the forces that defeated Napoleon at Waterloo in 1815. He became Prime Minister of the United Kingdom in 1825, and four years later oversaw the passing of the Catholic Emancipation Act which restored rights long denied to the Catholic majority on the island.

Begun in 1817, while Wellington was alive, the granite monument was finally completed in 1861, nine years after his death in 1852. Intended as a £20,000 city centre monument to Wellesley to commemorate his military victories, the original locations on either Merrion Square or St Stephen's Green met local opposition and it was instead built on the site of the salute battery in Phoenix Park. This battery had been used on ceremonial occasions to fire salutes so that the citizenry would be alerted to the occasion.

The funds to cover the cost of erecting the monument came from private subscriptions from Wellington's fellow countrymen. There were plans to include a statue of Wellesley on horseback but, once more, shortage of funds precluded that option.

The Phoenix Park rail tunnel travels beneath the monument where the line runs between Heuston and Connolly stations. The route is mostly used as a freight line.

The monument is famous amongst Dubliners for its eleven stone sloping steps, which, while easy to navigate on the upward journey, are a daunting task when descending from the base of the monument to ground level once more. Each of its four sides features

A spectacular aerial view of the Wellington Monument

bronze plaques cast from cannons captured at Waterloo. Three are pictorial representations of his career while the fourth bears an inscription. The plaques are: "Civil and Religious Liberty" by John Hogan; "Waterloo" by Thomas Farrell; and "The Indian Wars" by Joseph Kirk. The inscription on the city-facing side reads:

> Asia and Europe, saved by thee, proclaim
> Invincible in war thy deathless name,
> Now round thy brow the civic oak we twine
> That every earthly glory may be thine.

The monument features in James Joyce's novel *Finnegans Wake*, and has been a focal point for many public meetings in the park.

A sketch, by Pat Liddy, of one of the panels on the Wellington Monument

MEMORIAL GARDENS AT ISLANDBRIDGE

Across the Liffey on lands that once were included in Phoenix Park stands the War Memorial Gardens commemorating those Irish who fell in the First World War in the service of the British forces.

The Irish National War Memorial Trust was established in Dublin in July 1919 to provide a permanent memorial to the dead of the Great War which was fought from 1914 to 1918.

In the decades following this First World War, remembrance ceremonies for those who had died in British wars were held on 11 November at the Wellington Monument. Veterans and next of kin of the fallen would march up the quays from the city to the ceremony in Phoenix Park. From 1923 to 1933, an official representative of Saorstát Éireann attended the service in Phoenix Park.

On the day, the Guillemont Ginchy Cross was erected as a temporary cenotaph on which to focus ceremonies. The four-metre high wooden cross of Celtic design was made from an elm beam taken from a ruined French farmhouse and was originally erected between the Somme battlefields of Guillemont and Ginchy. From 1926 to 1938 it was positioned on one day each year in Phoenix Park at a point east of the Wellington Monument. The cross was subsequently placed in the newly established Irish National War Memorial Gardens at Islandbridge.

The Memorial Gardens, built at a cost of £56,000, became a centre of remembrance in Dublin from 1938. Designed by Sir Edwin Lutyens, the memorial commemorates the estimated 49,000 Irishmen who died and the estimated 300,000 who fought in the British army during the First World War. The garden was originally intended to be linked to the Military Road in Phoenix Park on the other side of the Liffey by a bridge, but this did not happen.

As participants of the war died off over the years, the gardens fell into disrepair. By 10 September 1988, restoration work undertaken by the Office of Public Works saw the gardens formally dedicated by representatives of the four main churches in Ireland and opened to the public, some fifty years after they were initially laid out. The park is maintained by the OPW as a place of remembrance.

HIBERNIAN MILITARY SCHOOL MEMORIAL

The Memorial Gardens can be seen clearly from the Military or Corkscrew Road inside the park, and particularly from the military Magazine Fort atop St Thomas's Hill. At the western end of this road and in the grounds of the present-day St Mary's Hospital stands a memorial to the "memory of the old boys of the Royal Hibernian Military School who laid down their lives for King and Country in the Great War of 1914–1918". Some eighty names are inscribed on the memorial.

The Royal Hibernian Military School was granted a royal charter and a site in Phoenix Park by George III. The present St Mary's Hospital was built in 1765 and for more than 150 years was known as the Royal Hibernian Academy. In the main, it provided for the education and care of children of British army personnel, some of whom had been killed in service, some of whom were posted overseas for extended periods. In turn, a number of their male children enrolled in the armed forces on reaching maturity and subsequently lost their own lives fighting in various wars for the Crown, and it is to them that the memorial is dedicated.

With the withdrawal of the British Forces in 1922 the "Hibernian" was transferred to Shorncliffe in England and was later absorbed into the Duke of York's Royal Military School near Dover.

KNOCKMARY CROMLECH

A monument of a different kind may be found atop the nearby Knockmary Hill where a cromlech is located beside the Park Ranger's Lodge. The Bronze Age burial cist dates from around 2,500 BC and was discovered in 1838 when landscaping work was being carried out under Decimus Burton, the landscape architect.

The workmen discovered four stone cists, each of which enclosed an urn of baked clay, ashes and bones. Two male skeletons that were discovered in the cist were removed to the National Museum of Ireland. A central stone chamber contained the skeletons, together with the burial artefacts. Seven stones are set in the ground in the form of an oval. Three stones, along with a modern concrete support, hold up the capstone, which is a limestone slab, about two metres long, a metre in breadth and thirty-four centimetres thick. The capstone was cracked by black frost damage in the winter of 1961. Such was the finish of the repairs that many have since, erroneously, ascribed the damage to vandalism.

The Cromlech at Knockmary

The heads of the skeletons were discovered pointing in a northerly orientation. The small area of the enclosure meant there was not sufficient room to allow the bodies to be fully outstretched. So it was necessary for them to be bent at the vertebrae or the lower joints. The skulls and teeth in both bodies were found to be in excellent condition, although they were more worn in one than in the other. Beneath each skull were found a large number of small shells, all of which conformed to the types of seashell to be found on the Irish coastline. Examination revealed that the shells had been pierced, and seemed to have been strung in the form of a necklace. A vegetable fibre found with the shells is believed to have been used to string the shells together.

PAPAL CROSS

A short distance away across the Fifteen Acres towers the Papal Cross, which recalls Pope John Paul II's visit to Ireland and Phoenix Park in September 1979 (see also Chapter 7). Some forty tonnes of steel were used to build the forty-one metre high cross at the top of a mound twelve metres above the surrounding ground. The altar rested on a stepped and carpeted timber platform of one acre. The cross and altar were designed by Scott Tallon Walker architects, who also co-ordinated the entire project at short notice. The firm was later contracted to provide advice on papal visits elsewhere.

It was originally planned that the cross would be removed after the visit; but following representations, it was decided to leave it stand as a permanent marker in the park landscape. For a while, there was a plan to develop an interpretative centre inside the mound below the cross, but this was not proceeded with. Instead, the nearby Ashtown Castle Visitor Centre offers a perspective on the day. The papal chair used by Pope John Paul II during the mass is on permanent display in the centre.

The Papal Cross

PIETÀ

A memorial of gratitude for the assistance offered to Italy by Ireland in the aftermath of the Second World War stands at the end of a long tree-lined walk in Áras an Uachtaráin. The Italian Government donated the sculpture *La Pietà* to the Irish State in 1947 to recall the relief supplies sent from Ireland during the post-war years of 1945–46. The 1930 Carrera marble sculpture was made by Ermenegildo Luppi, one of the foremost Italian sculptors, who died in 1937. The sculpture is nearly 2.5 metres high and weighs sixteen tonnes. The Italian community living in Ireland paid for its transportation and it was formally unveiled in the Rotunda of the National Museum in 1948, at a cost of something over £400.

It was later moved to a new site in the grounds of the Department of Education opposite the Pro Cathedral on Marlborough Street. The total cost of removing another monument to a different location, and erecting *La Pietà* in its place was more than £600, the Dáil was told in November 1955. However, the sculpture weathered badly in the forecourt of the building on Marlborough Street.

In August 2001, following restoration at a cost of some €330,000, the Commissioners of Public Works in Ireland arranged for the relocation of the sculpture to the Queen's Walk at Áras an Uachtárain, where it remains, protected by a lightweight canopy. The piece is now open on three sides with a solid wall forming the fourth side and is also protected among the trees of the gardens of the house. It can be viewed by guests at the house or by members of the public on guided tours of Áras an Uachtárain.

PHOENIX COLUMN

In the centre of the park stands the Phoenix Column or monument, said to recall the site of a spring of *fionn uisce*, or clear water, from which the park's name is thought to be derived. The column was but one of the many alterations undertaken by Philip Stanhope,

The Phoenix Column

the Earl of Chesterfield, when he took office as Lord Lieutenant. In 1731, Chesterfield swept away an existing wood and woodland clearing when he laid out a garden with plants and walls.

Chesterfield wished to commemorate the landscaping of the Phoenix Park and the fact that he later opened it formally to the people of Dublin as a public amenity, and so the monument came into being in 1747. He erected the Phoenix Column in the centre of what had been the clearing. The column was carved in Portland stone and bears the crest of the Earl of Chesterfield. The monument is often known locally as the Eagle Monument, because some Dubliners mistook the representation of the mythical bird atop the pillar for that of an eagle.

The monument was relocated to the main entrance of Áras an Uachtaráin in 1929 to allow for motor racing. Its return to the centre of the road in the 1980s created a roundabout, which had the effect of slowing modern commuter traffic and recreating a focal point from which many paths and roads lead to other attractions.

GARDA MEMORIAL

A memorial to members of the Garda Síochána killed on duty was unveiled at Garda Headquarters in Phoenix Park in 1966. The work was undertaken by sculptor Michael Biggs and stands inside the main entrance gates.

The Garda badge is included as a limestone coin set in granite with fully rounded bosses and a redesigned monogram in the centre. The badge is in the form of a Celtic cross. On the centrepiece are the intertwined initial letters of the Garda Síochána with the inscription "Garda Síochána na hÉireann" (Guardians of the Peace of Ireland).

The Garda Memorial

CARLISLE AND HEUSTON

Nowhere typifies the clash of jurisdictions and allegiances in Phoenix Park as much as the People's Flower Gardens, situated between the Parkgate Street Gate and North Circular Road Gate. At a spot close by the main road once stood a statue to the memory of George William Frederick Howard, the seventh Earl of Carlisle, in whose time the Gardens were opened to the public. Howard earned a reputation as a scholar and writer of graceful verse, obtaining in 1821 both the Chancellor's and the Newdigate prizes for a Latin and an English poem. Erected in 1870, the cost of his memorial was borne by public subscriptions. However, in the mid-twentieth century it was destroyed by an unauthorised explosion, leaving only the plinth remaining to this day.

Untouched, however, is a nearby bust of Sean Heuston, one of the executed leaders of the 1916 Rebellion. The Heuston piece is the work of Laurence Campbell of the Royal Irish Academy.

Heuston, a Dubliner, was employed as a clerk by the Great Southern and Western Railway Company. As a captain in the Volunteers, in Easter Week 1916 he was ordered by James Connolly to occupy the Mendicity Institution on the South Quay for three hours. He did so for three days before surrendering when surrounded by 500 British troops. He was shot in Kilmainham Jail on 8 May 1916, aged nineteen years of age, following a court martial. The railway station is named in his memory, as is the bridge beside the station on the way to Parkgate Street and the park.

Curiously, the statue is erected with Heuston's back to the railway and the city, thus facing away from Kilmainham where he ended his days. He is in fact facing Dublin Zoo. However, his image remains, unlike his poor neighbour Howard, who has departed the park in all material ways.

4

DEFENDING THE PARK
(AND THE NATION)

hoenix Park has a centuries-old association with both the
defence forces and the police in Ireland. From its early days
as a training ground for the British Army, right up to the
location there of the Department of Defence, the military presence
in the park has never been in doubt. Similarly, policing has long
been an essential part of Phoenix Park. The national police force,
Garda Síochána na hÉireann (Guardians of the Peace) has occupied
the training depot in the north-east corner of the park since the
force's foundation in 1922. Before that, the depot was home to the
Royal Irish Constabulary (RIC).

The defence of the nation and its citizens is therefore a core
function of the park. However, law and order in Phoenix Park itself
is maintained by a force of park rangers.

KEEPING ORDER IN THE PARK

The modern park is patrolled by park rangers, who were also
known as constables in a carry-over from the old British regime.
Rangers have the powers of a uniformed garda, if required in
special circumstances, but the national force aids and assists this

small local force at all times. Today, mobile patrols of rangers seek to ensure the safety and wellbeing of the park, its residents and visitors. However, the days of entering Phoenix Park with an armed guard are mercifully long gone. (Chapter 5 looks at the various crimes that have taken place over the centuries in the park.)

Under the 1925 Act that governs the park, the Commissioners of Public Works in Ireland "may appoint as many park constables, lodge-keepers, gate-keepers, officers, workmen and servants as the Commissioners shall, with the approval of the Minister, think necessary for the proper execution of the duties and exercise of the powers imposed or conferred on them in relation to the park by the Act".

Park rangers in uniform have the power of arrest, without warrant, in specified circumstances. However, whenever a park ranger makes an arrest, he must deliver that person into the

At the closing down of the city gate of Áras and Uachtaráin in 1989; Garda Paddy Monahan (Roscommon) and Ranger Jim Manning.

custody of a garda to be dealt with according to law, under the Act. For his part, a garda while on duty in the park has and may exercise the powers conferred on park constables by the 1925 Act in addition to any other power vested in him by law.

While a garda has the immediate protection of the force and the uniform in dealing with transgressors, the park ranger is protected mainly by law against attack whilst carrying out his duties. He may call for assistance in time of need but miscreants in the heat of the moment do not always recognise the powers vested in park constables. Assaulting a park ranger while engaged in the lawful execution of his duties or powers could lead to imprisonment for up to six months, on summary conviction.

Under the Phoenix Park Act 1925, the Garda Commissioner may also give directions to gardaí for enforcing preservation of order in the park and observance of regulations made under the Act. He may make regulations for routes to be observed by motor-cars, carriages, carts, and other vehicles, and by horses and persons in the park either generally or on special occasions. The fine is £5 (€6.35), but breaching a regulation is an offence and gives the Garda the right to remove transgressors from the park.

Such a regulation was made in June 1984 by Garda Commissioner Laurence Wren to cover the period of the official visit of US President Ronald Reagan to Ireland. The measure was directed at a small group of women who were gathered under the banner of Women for Disarmament and who were sitting on the grass within sight of the US Ambassador's residence at Deerfield. Wren's regulation prohibited specified activities within a radius of one mile of Deerfield, Phoenix Park, between the hours of 6.52 pm on 1 June 1984, and 3.00 pm on 4 June 1984, which was the scheduled duration of the Reagan visit to Ireland. Prohibited were: erection of temporary dwellings or shelters, or the carrying of placards, or signs that might result in a breach of the peace, in the opinion of the Garda. Also forbidden was congregation of persons pursuing a common objective that might result in public disorder, in the opinion of the Garda. Even acting in such a manner that might cause public anxiety, in the opinion of the Garda, was proscribed. Interfering with the free movement of the President of the United States through the area was also prohibited under the regulation.

The protestors were ejected from the park by a force of gardaí but returned nonetheless to resume picketing. Some thirty women were eventually arrested and held for some time before being brought before the courts, charged and remanded on bail for two weeks. They left the courts after Reagan had flown out of the country. In the event, the charges were dropped by the State and the regulation expired, according to a detailed account given by Gene Kerrigan in *Hard Cases: True Stories of Irish Crimes* (1996).

The 1925 Act confirmed a pre-independence 1919 set of regulations to be observed by constables, gatekeepers and deerkeepers of His Majesty's Phoenix Park, as signed into effect by J.J. Healy, Secretary to the Office of Public Works. These regulations included the admonition that all uniformed officers when on duty must keep themselves and their uniforms clean and neat in appearance. Uniforms were issued under the regulations as follows: one coat, one vest and two pairs of trousers, every eighteen months; one overcoat every three years; one uniform cap; two white cap covers; and one waterproof cap cover annually. Silk hats and gold bands were issued for gatekeepers at Dublin (Parkgate Street), North Circular Road, and Islandbridge Gates, annually. Two pairs of boots were issued every year, and waterproof capes, as required. White cap covers were to be worn on fine days from 1 May to 30 September inclusive. No officer was allowed to enter a public house while in uniform, as a matter of form.

While they were given new clothes on a scheduled basis, the recipients were to provide, from their older clothing stock, one or more reserve suits for rough work, during hard weather, or at night, or at such times as ordered by the Park Bailiff. An inspection of uniforms was made every three months.

Ranger Review in the 1930s. Back row left to right: Joe Buggy, Jack Manning, Jim Huston, Ned O'Brien, Bob Mooney, Barney McCormack, Dick Kinsella, George Willoughby. Front row left to right: Bob Lockwood, Jim Coyle, Charlie Simpson, Tom Newsome, Fred Fisher. The wrist stripes (front middle) represent the deerkeeper's rank. Taken in People's Flower Gardens in the 1930s at the monthly uniform inspection parade.

Rangers now wear all-weather high-visibility uniforms and hats suitable to their modern duties as motorised rangers.

During the hours on duty, constables were expected to range or to "keep moving" about the district assigned to them. Constable gatekeepers on the other hand were to remain outside their gate lodges and to have the gates open at 6.00 am from 10 February to November 15 and during the rest of the year, at 7.00 am. They were to be closed at nightfall for the safekeeping of the deer whose home it was and is, and for the safety of cattle taken in under licence during summer months to graze the grasslands. The gates were to be locked at 11.00 pm each night.

Cattle are no longer grazed in Phoenix Park for fear of contamination of the deer herd. During the 1950s, up to 1,000 head of cattle were allowed to graze in the park from 1 May to 1 November. The tariff was higher for older larger cattle than for younger animals. They were off-loaded at a special ramp beside Bessborough Lodge at Ashtown and a concrete base remains where the cattle were corralled while rangers Ned Lee and Jim Manning tagged and branded the animals for later inspection and identification. The branding with hot irons was carried out on the animals' hooves.

According to the 1919 regulations, the park gates were only to be opened again for the Lord Lieutenant, for the Chief Secretary, or Under-Secretary, or persons going to their residences with special permission, in writing. This naturally lapsed with the new order and nowadays the only access gates after 11.00 pm are Parkgate Street and Castleknock Gates.

A park constable could, under the old regime, arrest and give in charge to the nearest Dublin Metropolitan Policeman anybody found committing serious offences. Such offences included theft, personal assault, indecent exposure, or wilful damage. A DMP barracks was located, conveniently enough, at the entrance to the park at Parkgate Street. The barracks became a sub-station of Cabra Garda station which was itself located beside the laundry Lodge at the rear of Áras an Uachtaráin. The DMP barracks closed in 1930 and the structure is now in ruins. Cabra station moved outside the walls when a new station was built on the Navan Road in the mid-twentieth century.

Not only were gatekeepers required to be neat and tidy, they were to keep their own areas under care. Gatekeepers were to be particular in sweeping the area around the gates every morning before they put on uniform.

With the exception of the lights at the main Parkgate Street entrance and at North Circular Road, gatekeepers themselves were required to light and extinguish and keep perfectly clean the gate lamps in connection with their respective gates. The lamps were to be lighted shortly before dusk and extinguished at 11.00 pm, all year round. However, Lamp No. 48 on Castleknock Gate was not to be extinguished until daybreak, according to the regulations, it being an illumination of a gate that remained open through the night.

POLICE IN THE PARK

In the eighteenth century, Dublin city was bounded by the North and South Circular Roads, the contemporary equivalent of modern motorways designed to carry traffic around rather than through a city. Construction of two canals reinforced the city limits, which became defined as that area lying between the two canals. The South Circular Road begins or ends opposite the Islandbridge turnstile of Phoenix Park while the North Circular Road ends up, not surprisingly, at the North Circular Road Gate of Phoenix Park.

So, when a 1786 law was passed in an effort to reform Dublin's police service, Phoenix Park was included in the Dublin Metropolitan District. That district included the land inside the circular roads, and the land inside the walls of Phoenix Park. To this day, Phoenix Park comes under the jurisdiction of Dublin City Council for planning purposes, because its main entrance is on Parkgate Street.

From its formation in 1836 up to 1922, the Dublin Metropolitan Police Force, or DMP, with their distinctive pointed helmets, functioned as an unarmed force. Responsibility for the force was taken over by the Free State Government then and it was re-named Póilíní Áth Cliath. The DMP was amalgamated with the new Garda Síochána force in April 1925 and moved to Phoenix Park from its own depot in Kevin Street at the rear of St Patrick's Cathedral, where a modern Garda station now stands. The pointed helmets were replaced by the familiar flat cap of today in the early 1930s.

While the new metropolitan district was being laid out in Dublin, law and order in general around the country was maintained by constables and watchmen employed by local authorities, supported by British military forces.

Chief Secretary Robert Peel sponsored a law in 1816 creating a basic police force organised along paramilitary lines. In 1836, county and provincial constabularies were merged into a centralised constabulary of Ireland. The Irish Constabulary was later awarded the prefix Royal by Queen Victoria for suppressing the Fenian Rising in 1867.

Phoenix Park was chosen as the most suitable central location for the new force's main depot and by the end of 1839, Jacob Owen of the Office of Public Works in Ireland had completed plans for a barracks to cost some £10,000 to develop.

The main buildings were occupied by 1842. A gravel parade ground was added for drilling and review purposes. A riding school for the mounted constabulary was built in 1845. The Depot provided accommodation for 100 officers and 200 other ranks. The barracks formed three sides of a rectangular parade ground. The main north front, with a clock in the middle, contained officers' quarters and mess-room, sleeping rooms for the infantry and the commandant's quarters. On the east or city side was built a short wing for infantry and the commandant's office; on the west, or park side, similar accommodation was provided, with stabling beneath for cavalry.

The original Burton-designed sunken perimeter fence terminated at each end of the Depot at a rustic cottage guard-house. However, the sunken fence, which adhered to Decimus Burton's overall design for fencing in Phoenix Park, was eventually replaced by the present railings.

A red-bricked row of small living quarters for single men was provided between the Depot perimeter and North Circular Road lodge. Men had to vacate the property on marriage.

A school was converted for use as a chapel in 1923 when the depot was occupied by the new Garda force. It was later used as a recreation hall, and then became the band room of the Garda band. The old officers' mess became the Garda Officers' Club.

The first Depot drill instructor was Londoner Thomas Fleming, who had joined the Rifle Brigade at age fifteen. At age forty-two, in 1842, he was appointed the first Head Constable Major of the Depot. Under his organisation the first cadet officer training police depot for the British Empire was established in Phoenix Park.

As the country quieted somewhat, at least temporarily, at the dawn of the twentieth century, police constables from many parts of the British Empire travelled to Dublin to participate in training courses. From 1907 to 1912 colonial police officers received their cadet training in Dublin and the guidelines taught in Phoenix Park were brought back to other countries to form basic structures of policing. According to Garda records, the February 1912 issue of the *RIC Magazine* reported: "There was seen on the Depot square

Sentry duty at the RIC Depot, circa 1910

the spectacle . . . of coloured and white Policemen drilling side-by-side." From 1907 to 1912 cadet training was provided in the park to officers from Nigeria (47 cadets); Kenya (15); Ghana (12); Uganda (11); Trinidad (6); Guiana (5); Jamaica (4); Sierra Leone (3); Gambia (2); and to others from elsewhere. "All had to wear the uniform of their respective colonies, and never was such a variety of uniforms seen at the Depot before," said the report.

However, training of policemen for other parts of the British Empire drew to a close when the new administration of the Irish Free State took over in 1922. The paramilitary Royal Irish Constabulary was disbanded in 1922 and by the end of the year they had evacuated their home of eighty years in Phoenix Park to make room for the newly formed force of the Garda Síochána.

The new unarmed force followed on from the RIC, but assumed the rank structure of the Dublin Metropolitan Police. The DMP operated as an independent body even after the foundation of the State in 1922, before being incorporated into the Garda Síochána in 1925. In that year, the DMP became the Dublin Metropolitan Division (DMD) of the Garda Síochána.

Policing can place a garda in many different situations. Murder is thankfully a rare occurrence in the park, despite the high profile given to earlier killings, as described in Chapter 5. However, uniformed gardaí do not carry firearms. This has been the situation since 1922 when the first commissioner, Michael Staines, said: "The Garda Síochána will succeed not by force of arms or numbers, but on their moral authority as servants of the people."

Commissioner Staines held office for only eight months. It was his successors, Eoin O'Duffy and Eamon Broy, who played central roles in the development of the force. O'Duffy later became infamous as the short-lived Irish neo-fascist founder and leader of the politically motivated "Blueshirts", before sailing to Spain in the 1930s to fight on the side of Franco's Nationalists in the Spanish Civil War. Broy's fame grew in the 1990s when he featured in the film *Michael Collins* as a double agent in Dublin Castle. However, though the screen Broy was killed by British forces during the War of Independence, in reality, Broy headed the Garda Síochána from 1933 to 1938. He died in 1972, at the age of eighty-five years.

In 1923, Phoenix Park Depot was occupied by the new force led by O'Duffy, its second Commissioner. Thereafter, the Depot was used as a combined headquarters and training centre until a separate headquarters was established across the Liffey valley at the Royal Hospital, Kilmainham. When that fell into decay, the Garda Commissioner and his staff returned in the early 1950s to Phoenix Park. More recently, to cope with modern demand, a four-storey extension to Garda Headquarters was completed in 1987 at a cost of €5.7 million.

Following the return of the top brass in the 1950s, it became necessary to provide either a new headquarters or a separate training centre. It was decided to move the training facility to a new location. In 1964 a training centre was established in the old McCann military barracks at Templemore, County Tipperary, and that section of the Depot structure is now called the Garda College.

Garda Headquarters today

In recognising the dangers of being an unarmed force, self-defence forms an important part of basic training at the Garda College for new recruits. All officers on patrol carry handcuffs and a baton for use against violent disorder. In addition, detective gardaí may carry firearms while working in plain clothes. These members are available as armed backup for their uniformed colleagues, whenever need arises.

Music and policing go hand in hand, it seems. In 1861, an RIC band had been established in the Depot. The Government stipulated that its numbers should not exceed forty-five, but as it happened, only twenty-six musicians were enrolled under the first bandmaster. The band prospered and thrived and, in addition to providing appropriate music in the Depot on passing-out days, was much in demand in wider society for special events.

A Garda Band was established shortly after the foundation of the force itself and gave its first public performance on Easter Monday 1923. Not confined to being a marching band, under the direction of the first bandmaster, Superintendent DJ Delaney, a céilí band, a pipe band and a dance orchestra were all formed from within its ranks. Dancing must have been a popular pastime for the Guardians of the Peace! In 1938, the Dublin Metropolitan Garda Band (then based at Kevin Street) and the Garda Band amalgamated and the combined band was based at the Depot.

In 1964, the band toured the USA and Canada. However, the following year it was disbanded, to general dismay, for budgetary reasons. It was re-established in 1972 to celebrate the fiftieth anniversary of the foundation of An Garda Síochána and has been much in demand for all sorts of occasions ever since.

Sometimes, wheels turn full circle in policing, as in life. The old disbanded RIC mounted units were eventually succeeded by the Garda Mounted Unit which commenced operational duty on 17 May 1998 as a national resource. The present strength of the unit is two sergeants, sixteen gardaí and fourteen horses. The unit headquarters are located, not at Garda Headquarters, but

*Members of the Garda Mounted Unit outside their
headquarters at Áras an Uachtaráin*

in the grounds of the nearby Áras an Uachtaráin. Facilities there include fifteen finely appointed stables, tack rooms, a forge, feed and bedding stores, an all-weather training arena and paddocks. At times, and when public order may be threatened, or during ceremonial duties and special events, mounted officers patrol in Phoenix Park, recalling earlier times in the park when the tempo of life was somewhat slower than it is today.

The unit concentrates exclusively on horses of the Irish draught breed. It has been the force's experience that the breed has the temperament and physical qualities most desirable in a police horse. The Irish draught horse had almost become redundant as a consequence of the fall-off in commercial demand for draught animals over recent decades. However, according to the Garda, there could be no greater use for the animal than its current policing role.

A Garda and police museum was established in the Depot, and a Garda Síochána Historical Society was later formed. The year 1997 saw the seventy-fifth anniversary of the founding of the Garda Síochána, and the museum and the historical society encouraged participation by all in activities touching on the history and development of policing in Ireland, and in particular An Garda Síochána. In the same year, the museum moved from Phoenix Park to its present location at the Records Tower in Dublin Castle. Amongst the detail to be found in the museum is an explanation as to why the RIC uniform was rifle green in colour. It was in fact based on the Rifle Brigade uniform, according to retired Garda Jim Herlihy, whose book *The Royal Irish Constabulary* was published in 1997 by Four Courts Press. Herlihy recalled men being taught the science of drill at the Depot and how they were to march past with heads erect, but not thrown back, without the benefit of any musical accompaniment. The RIC standard arms were a short carbine with a spring bayonet. Many service records for the RIC and the DMP are available though the museum. Service record details can be obtained from the Garda museum and archives section, with some advance notice, by phone on 00-353-(0)1-6669998 or by email to gatower@iol.ie. Visitors are welcome to call in to inspect the exhibits and to consult the curator and archivist, Sergeant Pat McGee, between 9.00 am and 5.00 pm, Monday to Friday, or otherwise by appointment. A website at www.policehistory.com is the online presence of the Garda Síochána Historical Society, where further detail on the force and its development beyond Phoenix Park may be found.

As the unified national police service, the Garda exercises all police functions in the country. There are no areas where the writ of the national force does not run. The force provides State security services and all criminal and traffic law enforcement functions are performed by it.

While the Minister for Justice is responsible to the Government for the performance of An Garda Síochána, he does not run the organisation on a day-to-day basis. This is the function of the Commissioner, who discharges his responsibilities from headquarters in Phoenix Park.

Through times of stress and turmoil, the depot in Phoenix Park has played a crucial role in policing both the park and the wider community. Resources have been readily provided by the State to allow it to continue to do so, if the astonishing gaffe of disbanding the high-profile Garda band is discounted.

MILITARY MATTERS

A large flat expanse on a plateau above the capital city was always going to attract the military mind, especially if the city's river flowed below the plateau and soldiers' barracks could be built nearby.

The 200 or so flat acres of grassland at the centre of Phoenix Park has been the scene of army manoeuvres, camps, reviews, charging horses and cavalrymen shouting huzzah at the Queen of England and at assembled high society. Where the Wellington Monument now stands, there was once a salute battery in place for formal occasions and royal birthdays when the cannon were fired to remind all and sundry that the military was standing by for all occasions, both joyous and sombre, lest they forget.

On the other hand, hungry soldiers serving under Charles II in the seventeenth century poached pheasant and partridge to supplement their official rations. So, a soldier's life in Phoenix Park was not all beer and skittles and galloping horses.

With the posting to Dublin of an ever-increasing number of regiments in the eighteenth century, two hospitals were built for the exclusive use of the army. One was at Arbour Hill and the other, the Royal Military Infirmary, was built on Infirmary Road, but inside the wall of Phoenix Park, in the south-east angle of the

Park overlooking the People's Flower Gardens. The building was completed in 1788 at a cost of £9,000. It is a structure of Portland stone with a frontage of 170 feet. The centre has a handsome cupola and clock. The first patients arrived at the large and airy Infirmary in 1790.

By 1910, the building had become outdated and a new hospital, St Bricin's, was commissioned on the site of the old structure at Arbour Hill. Patients transferred there from the Royal Infirmary in 1913. The empty infirmary was taken over by British Army Headquarters, Irish Command, who vacated the Royal Hospital, Kilmainham, where it had been stationed for more than 150 years. In May 1923, the General Headquarters of the Free State Army moved to the Royal Infirmary at Phoenix Park and has, in one form or other, remained there ever since — the building now houses the offices of the Department of Defence, which is also out-of-bounds to public visitation.

It was in fact from British army headquarters at Phoenix Park that operations were directed by the Commander-in-Chief, Major General French, against the insurgents of 1916. The rebel leader Patrick Pearse was taken there to sign the unconditional surrender of the insurgents on 29 April.

In the preceding nineteenth century, military reviews in the park were attended by hundreds of thousands of people there to see regimental bands, marching soldiers, charging cavalry and artillery firing blanks, to the delight of the attendance. In 1844, some 5,000 men of the garrison of Dublin took part in one such event. Contemporary reports said the infantry formed squares for an attack on the enemy cavalry, with the artillery firing away to the sides.

Perched above the corkscrew road above the Liffey valley and overlooking the western approach to the city is the star-shaped Magazine Fort, on St Thomas' Hill above Islandbridge. Built in 1735 on the site of the original Phoenix House, the Magazine was designed for arms and explosive storage for the Dublin-based

Aerial view of the star-shaped Magazine Fort

regiments. Armed guards were posted to keep care of the army's stores in the park.

Nonetheless, in the twentieth century, it was the focus of two raids by republicans, whose members were seeking arms or trying to neutralise the weapons held within.

The Irish Volunteers, who gave the modern army its cap-badge and buttons, was formed at a public meeting at the Rotunda Rooms, at the top of O'Connell Street, in Dublin on 25 November 1913, when some 8,000 people from a wide cross-section of backgrounds created an Irish Army by acclamation.

In Easter 1915, some 27,000 Volunteers paraded in front of their leader John Redmond in Phoenix Park. However, his encouragement to them to serve in the British army overseas marked the beginning of the end of the movement as constituted. What remained became a separatist force from which came many of the rebels of Easter week 1916.

It was during the week of the Easter rebellion that the first raid on the Magazine Fort took place. A party of Irish Volunteers took the fort and retreated, having set a fire to blow the place up, but their short-lived initiative failed when the fire went out.

The Volunteers were succeeded, in 1919, by the Irish Republican Army (IRA), the guerrilla organisation that fought the War of Independence. Shortly after the creation of the 1922 Irish Free State, the IRA was succeeded by the modern Defence Forces, whose headquarters remain at Phoenix Park.

The Irish title Óglaigh na hÉireann, which had previously been used by both the Irish Volunteers and the IRA, was adopted by the Defence Forces as a claim of continuity with these organisations. However, anti-treaty activists who were members of the IRA that fought for independence and who decided to fight on declined to yield the title of Óglaigh na hÉireann to the new State forces. In modern times, active IRA members in Northern Ireland have referred to themselves as volunteers and members of Óglaigh na hÉireann.

In fact, both claimants to the name faced one another at the Magazine Fort in the park on 23 December 1939 when the Fort was raided for the second time. The Irish Army was by then holding munitions in the Magazine. A few days before Christmas that year IRA lookouts were posted at the Islandbridge Gates while a convoy of forty lorries was brought in to remove ammunition, rifles and machine-guns. Such was the swift response from the Defence Forces to the theft of their stored weapons that all Christmas leave was cancelled and, by 28 December, most of the stolen equipment had been recovered by the army, mainly from dumps in the midlands. Two IRA men were arrested in the park at the time of the raid and when the recovery operation was over it was realised that more weaponry than was stolen had been recovered such was the diligence of the search.

Today, the fort is designated as a List 1 building in the Dublin City Development Plan, and has been empty for some years. Interestingly, in 2005, reports circulated in the media that the Magazine Fort, which is in state ownership, could serve as a setting for a new Abbey Theatre, or an opera house. The proposal came with the information that the park, being on a spur from the M50, the twentieth century's city bypass, could be accessed without meeting Dublin city centre traffic. Considerable car parking facilities were already in place near the Papal Cross, and this was advanced as a site that deserved serious consideration. Quite how patrons were to get from the car park on a windy night in November across the Fifteen Acres was not explained.

They might have heard the ghostly sound of young men digging mock trenches in preparation for the real-life trenches of the Great War where many were to lose their lives. Not far away from Wellington Monument, young soldiers from the Royal Dublin Fusiliers practised digging and using trenches in preparation for their departure to the European front of the First World War. Many did not return and the park grass grew over their imitation fortifications.

In the 1940s, when invasion threatened, the Irish army even placed obstructions on the flatland of Fifteen Acres and on the four-kilometre stretch of Chesterfield Avenue to prevent the landing of an invading enemy's planes and armed forces. Protruding railway sleepers were buried in the ground and netting was strung across Chesterfield Avenue. Gun emplacements were installed in St Mary's Hospital to ward off attack, and the American Ambassador's residence across the open space was similarly protected by emplaced guns. An airborne invading force could quite quickly have overrun both police and military headquarters, both of which were, and are, located near to one another in Phoenix Park. Munitions were to be found and destroyed at the Magazine Fort and a short distance away were the three military barracks of Collins, Clancy and McKee. Collins Barracks is now part of the National Museum; Clancy Barracks was sold in 2001 for private housing development; but

McKee Barracks is still in use. Its rear entrance opens onto Phoenix Park on the Back Road at a spot beside Garda Headquarters.

The military presence in Phoenix Park remains to this day. Headquarters for the Irish Defence Forces and the Department of Defence occupy the old Infirmary and a small area inside the eastern wall of Phoenix Park. The Irish Defence Forces incorporates air, sea and land forces and operates in support of the Garda Síochána and sometimes are called on to do so in Phoenix Park on official duty.

One recent occasion when the army was deployed was on 1 May 2004 when the leaders of the expanding European Union came calling to Farmleigh House, with attendant protestors. Soldiers were mainly deployed at Farmleigh and on the periphery road inside Phoenix Park. A temporary restricted flight area was in place over Dublin and the Air Defence regiment provided air cover for Farmleigh, the park and other areas. For the May Day events the army deployed 2,700 troops and associated equipment in the park during the security operation. In 2004, the Irish Army consisted of 8,500 service members, supplemented by reserves.

A park resident is even supreme commander of the Defence Forces. The ruling President holds the nominal position; but the powers are exercised on the advice of the Government. A constitutional crisis arose in October 1976 which led to the resignation and departure from the park of the then President Cearbhall Ó Dálaigh, involving the Minister for Defence, and a speech given by the Minister to officers in an army mess. Defence Minister Paddy Donegan TD referred to President Ó Dálaigh's refusal to sign tough anti-crime legislation as a "thundering disgrace". The Taoiseach, Liam Cosgrave TD, subsequently refused Donegan's resignation. In the constitutional crisis that followed, Ó Dálaigh resigned as President of Ireland and was succeeded by Patrick J. Hillery.

The army, in addition to having its headquarters facing on to Infirmary Road, maintains athletic grounds in the park for sporting and orienteering activities. Indeed, the army athletic grounds in

Phoenix Park, located near to the Dog Pond, is used as a modern landing pad for air-sea rescue helicopters ferrying patients to Dublin hospitals. (Under the Phoenix Park Act 1925, no person other than members of the Defence Forces or of the Garda Síochána may themselves train or drill or be trained or drilled in the use of arms, or practise gymnastics or any military exercises or manoeuvres in the park.)

In addition to the regular army, the headquarters of Civil Defence is located at Ratra House, the former Private Secretary's Lodge currently used as combined headquarters and training depot. From 1926–1940, Ratra was occupied by the Adjutant General of the Irish Army. Civil Defence was set up in 1950 to be part of the national defence structure as a civil response to hazards that might arise in a war situation. The Civil Defence School was formally opened at Ratra in June 1951. With the enactment of the Civil Defence Act 2002, the Civil Defence Board assumed responsibility for civil defence at national level. Under government decentralisation plans Civil Defence headquarters was scheduled to move to Roscrea, County Tipperary, in 2005. However, as with much of the decentralisation plan designed to move government offices out of Dublin, this part of the plan is delayed and for the moment, Civil Defence for the nation and for Phoenix Park remains in the park.

Indeed, a casual walker in the park may come across park rangers patrolling the park in modern vehicles, encounter a Garda on horseback from the Mounted Unit, or just as easily meet a soldier in full pack uniform running along a track as part of a strenuous training exercise.

All are part of keeping the park and the nation safe for posterity and for the people.

5

CRIMES AND MISDEMEANOURS

Wherever people gather there will be an attraction for criminals to attend with the intent of enriching themselves at the expense of others. Phoenix Park is a large area with many secluded spots and if someone is intent on doing wrong it is quite possible they can do so without being readily detected.

However, law enforcement will usually catch up with them and prison sentences ensue. In earlier centuries the hangman's noose was a villain's fate; nowadays, jail time beckons, and that can be for a very long time indeed, as the murderous Malcolm McArthur discovered in 1982 to his cost.

HIGHWAYMEN AND DUELLISTS

In times past, it was quite normal for people of substance to be accompanied by armed escorts as they made their way through Phoenix Park. The Viceroy, the king's representative in Ireland, travelled with a mounted guard of cavalry to protect his body and his office at all times. Many others chose to be similarly protected on their way through the park.

Trouble and danger could begin as soon as the entrance gate was passed through. The area inside Castleknock Gate, for instance, on the western perimeter of the park and at the top end of Chesterfield

Avenue, was a particularly dangerous place for the unwary. Inside the gates is an area known as Butchers' Woods which at one time was a heavily wooded area spreading both north and south of the gate. In these trees it was well recognised that highwaymen would await the arrival of unwary travellers on their way into the city. The highwaymen would accost the hapless travellers and relieve them of whatever value they carried. Some escaped with their lives, if they were fortunate.

The woods, however, were not named for the blackguardism that took place there, but rather for the mayhem caused when butchers from the city markets gathered amongst the trees to settle disputes. Butchers' Woods is thought to have taken its name from the time when it was the place of pitched battles and duels and fights between members of the butcher's guilds that were then common in the meat markets of Dublin. More serious disputes and arguments were taken to the park and fought out in ritualised battles with tools of the butchering trade.

In the nineteenth century, the park, and its review ground, as the Fifteen Acres was also called, became a popular place for duels between men of breeding who believed their honour demanded respect by another. Some lost their lives as a consequence, or took their opponents'. Duelling seems to have been tolerated, at least when passers-by weren't being wounded by stray shots. In his book *The Phoenix Park*, currently out of print, author Kenneth MacGowan recalled complaints being made by citizens of the time concerning the danger to them of stray bullets from such duels. So while honour may have been paramount in the minds of the protagonists, their sense of direction might not have been all that might have been desired.

According to MacGowan, the most famous duel to take place in the park was between Sir Jonah Barrington and Leonard McNally. McNally subsequently became even more famous for betraying the United Irishman leader Lord Edward Fitzgerald to the authorities, in May 1798. In any case, in the park, pistols were handed out to

Barrington and McNally and nine paces were taken, followed by the sound of two pistol shots. McNally suffered a slight thigh abrasion and Barrington found the skirt of his coat to be perforated on both sides. A scratch from a passing bullet had marked his thighs. In the event, the pair decided honour was satisfied and repaired to the city to fight another day.

THE INVINCIBLES MURDERS

Earl Spencer was Viceroy when revolutionary violence came very close to the Vice Regal Lodge. Spencer arrived in Ireland in May 1882, accompanied by the new Chief Secretary, Lord Frederick Cavendish. After a meeting with officials in Dublin Castle, Spencer returned to the Lodge, accompanied by a mounted escort. Cavendish, however, who knew Dublin well, opted to walk to Phoenix Park to attend a dinner with the Viceroy later that evening. Under-Secretary, Thomas Burke, catching up on Cavendish, alighted from a horse-drawn cab to walk with him.

Within sight of the Vice Regal Lodge, the men were stabbed to death with surgical knives by members of the Invincibles, a small revolutionary group of the period. Oliver St John Gogarty, in his autobiography *As I Was Going Down Sackville Street* (1937), said one of the knives used was in fact an amputation knife. Such was the violence of the stabbings that Spencer heard their death shrieks from his room in the Vice Regal Lodge.

The killers mounted an open car and made off in the direction of Chapelizod Gates to the south. The bodies of the two men were brought to Dr Steevens's Hospital near Kingsbridge railway station (now Heuston), not far from Parkgate Street where so recently they had fallen into step on their way to the Lodge. The corpses were placed under guard, pending an inquest.

Proclamations were issued offering rewards of up to £10,000 for information which would lead to an arrest. Eight months later, in January 1883, warrants were issued for the arrest of more than twenty men who were subsequently tried for the killing. All were convicted and six received the death sentence, while the others were given long terms of imprisonment.

Hanged at Kilmainham between May and June 1883 were Daniel Curley, Michael Fagan, Patrick Delany, Thomas Caffrey, Joseph Brady and Tim Kelly. Oliver St John Gogarty recorded that Marwood, the executioner, miscalculated the death drop of Joe Brady and had to go down into the execution pit to hold on to Brady's legs until he expired.

Another man died on 29 July 1883 as a result of the murders. Crown witness James Carey was killed on a ship off Cape Town when Patrick O'Donnell, a member of the Invincibles, who had followed him from Ireland, carried out a sentence of death placed on him by the organisation when he turned queen's evidence against his former companions. Carey had claimed, to no avail, that investigating police had tricked him into giving evidence. Carey was granted a royal pardon after the trials and set out on the *Melrose Castle*, a steamer bound for South Africa, and a new life, but he never arrived there. O'Donnell, in turn, was tried for killing Carey and, on 17 November, executed.

At the time of the murders of Cavendish and Burke, Home Rule for Ireland was being discussed in the Westminster parliament and the killings set back the cause of Irish self-government by some distance, such was the reaction in Britain and Ireland.

The exact location of the murders is a matter of debate to this day. However, some nationalist historians mark the supposed spot beside Chesterfield Avenue each year with a small cross cut into the grass.

MALCOLM McARTHUR

Chesterfield Avenue was the scene of another horrific murder almost exactly a century after the Invincibles murders, when Bridie Gargan, a young nurse who was sunbathing beside her parked car, was beaten to death with a lump hammer by a would-be bank robber intent on stealing her car. The crime was to have national consequences and result in a very long prison term for the killer.

Gargan lived in a one-bedroomed apartment in nearby Castleknock. On the afternoon of 22 July 1982, the twenty-nine-year-old nurse had come off duty and was relaxing in the sun beside Chesterfield Avenue. Aristocratic Meath man-about-town Malcolm McArthur attacked her with a lump hammer when she tried to stop him taking her car.

A gardener at the nearby US Ambassador's residence hurried over to try to save the young woman. He tackled her assailant at the car, but McArthur had bundled his bloodied victim into her silver metallic Renault 5 and drove off down the wide footpath of the park, despite attempts to stop him. The gardener unsuccessfully attempted to get passing motorists to stop for assistance, and eventually alerted the Garda to what had happened, by phone from the residence.

McArthur, who was not a skilled driver, drove down the since-closed Khyber Road and exited the park at Islandbridge gate. A passing ambulance driver, seeing the bloodied body in the speeding car, thought the victim had been in an accident and led the way to St James Hospital, ironically where the unfortunate victim had been working that day. McArthur drove behind the wailing ambulance but abandoned the car and Nurse Gargan's body on arrival at the hospital.

The subsequent manhunt ended bizarrely at the home of the serving Attorney General Patrick Connolly some weeks later when McArthur was arrested. McArthur was by then a house guest of Connolly. Connolly was unaware of McArthur's crime, but opted to leave the country on pre-arranged holidays, even though he was the state's chief law officer. However, Connolly cut the holiday short and returned to Ireland following discussions with Taoiseach Charles Haughey TD.

When Haughey was asked for comment on McArthur's place of capture, he said that in normal circumstances the attorney general would be the person a Taoiseach would turn to for advice in the matter. He said the sequence of events was "grotesque, unbelievable, bizarre and unprecedented". The acronym GUBU subsequently came into the language to describe a series of unconnected events having a cumulative effect beyond anybody's control. Connolly later resigned his position as attorney general.

Nurse Gargan was not McArthur's only victim. McArthur shot dead Donal Dunne, an Edenderry farmer, some days after he killed Gargan. Dunne had advertised a shotgun for sale in the newspaper and agreed to meet McArthur, who had responded to the ad. Bizarrely, McArthur killed Dunne and made off with the gun, even though Dunne had wished to dispose of the weapon through a mutually agreed sale. There was no question of him refusing to hand over the gun, since he had advertised it for sale.

McArthur pleaded guilty to Nurse Gargan's murder. A second charge of murdering Donal Dunne was dropped and a nolle prosequi entered by the State, to voluble protests from Dunne's family who subsequently gathered signatures to a public petition seeking McArthur's prosecution for the second murder, but to no avail. McArthur was sentenced to life for the killing of Bridie Gargan in 1982 and was still incarcerated in 2005, some twenty-three years later.

In a strange twist of fate, when McArthur's application for parole came up for review some twenty years later the serving Minister for Justice was Michael McDowell TD, who had served as a junior counsel on McArthur's defence team during his trial. McDowell passed the file to his junior minister Willie O'Dea TD to consider when presented with the request for parole. McArthur served twenty years of his life sentence in Mountjoy before being moved to the open prison at Shelton Abbey in May 2003 to prepare for any eventual release, on the advice of the Parole Board.

A Vicious Assault

The main road of Phoenix Park was to be witness, some years later, to another horrific attack carried out on innocent parties who were unknown to their assailants. While political assassination can be understood on some level for what it is, however misguided, the taking of a life when somebody resists being robbed takes theft to new depths.

Two German backpackers arrived in the park in August 1991 and, as twilight gave way to darkness, settled down for what they thought would be a peaceful night's sleep under canvas in a small copse beside Chesterfield Avenue and within shouting distance of Áras an Uachtaráin. Unfortunately for them, a four-man gang of local thieves happened on them in the woods. The attackers capsized the tent, and their assaults on the visitors included the use of thumbs thrust into their eyeballs, according to reports of the incident. The victims were severely beaten with stout sticks and left where they lay. By the time the attack ended, one of the visitors, Georg Plappert, lay dead and the other, Roland Sewen, was battered almost to death sustaining severe head injuries and permanently losing sight in one eye. In the event, the gang made off with a sum of £30 (€38).

The State Pathologist said later that that the dead man's injuries were among the worst he had seen in seventeen years of dealing with the results of violent crime. The survivor of the assault, Ronald Sewen, was able to assist investigating gardaí in identifying the perpetrators of the attack. The assailants were arrested shortly afterwards. Though four men attacked the unsuspecting visitors, just two were charged. Two other suspects were not charged because of technicalities relating to the investigation. The two Dublin men later sentenced to jail for the vicious assault were Paul McDonagh, who received ten years for his part in the brutal attack, and John Francis McAllister, who was jailed for eight years. McAllister had sixty-six previous convictions, including some for violence.

OTHER CRIMES

While Phoenix Park is large and violence could occur anywhere, the most serious crimes have occurred beside Chesterfield Avenue, ironically the busiest road in the park.

In 2001, carpenter Gerard Kelly (30) from Leixlip, County Kildare, was jailed for seven years for raping a prostitute at the polo grounds on Chesterfield Avenue. Presiding judge, Mr Justice Paul Carney, heard in the Central Criminal Court that the woman was paid £20 (€25) by Kelly for a sex act. However, Kelly then assaulted the woman while the act was in progress, the court was told. He was caught when the victim memorised the registration number of his van and reported the attack to the Garda. He initially defended himself by saying the woman had tried to rob him. However, he pleaded guilty in court.

The park also saw the ending of two kidnappings in the last century. Lord and Lady Donoughmore, who had been kidnapped by an IRA gang, were released in Phoenix Park at 3.00 am on 7 June 1974. IRA bombers Dolours and Marian Price had been on hunger strike in Brixton prison in England and the elderly Donoughmores were taken as hostages from their home in County Tipperary as surety against their release. Two other IRA prisoners, Frank Stagg and Michael Gaughan, had already died on hunger strike in Parkhurst prison. In the event, the Price sisters ended their strike on 7 June, and the Donoughmores were driven to Phoenix Park by their kidnappers. They were let out of the kidnapper's car and told to walk in a straight line without looking back, while the car drove away. They eventually came to a house and knocked on the door seeking assistance.

At least their release was peaceful, unlike the case of a notorious Dublin criminal who was abducted by an IRA unit in a snatch that went badly wrong for the kidnappers in the 1990s. Gardaí apprehended a number of the kidnappers following a car chase during which shots were fired. The kidnap van eventually halted at the top of steps leading down to the stile at Islandbridge, and the kidnappers were arrested.

Major crimes apart, the park, as with any large area, can be the scene of unprovoked crimes. Modern car hijackings are not unknown as lone occupants, usually male, pull into recognised and secluded areas for contact with male prostitutes and are sometimes approached by cheery male thieves, who make off with their cars and their dignity. In other cases violent assaults have left the victims in the embarrassing situation of explaining to friends and family their presence at that time in a darkened public park.

But for most people Phoenix Park is a safe area to enjoy most of the time and help from rangers or gardaí is never far away when called for.

6

LITERARY LINKS

Phoenix Park, like so many of Ireland's other landmarks, has its fair share of literary links, from Sheridan Le Fanu and Oliver St John Gogarty right up to Seamus Heaney in the twenty-first century.

SHERIDAN LE FANU

The park's long literary tradition reaches back at least to the nineteenth century when a young Sheridan Le Fanu lived in the Hibernian Academy, where St Mary's Hospital now stands.

Le Fanu's pioneering work in gothic horror has been eclipsed somewhat by his better-known contemporary, Dublin writer Bram Stoker, whose 1897 novel *Dracula* has never been out of print, and which has spawned many imitators. However, a reading of Le Fanu's 1872 vampire novella *Carmilla*, which predates Stoker's blood-drenched *Dracula* by a quarter of a century, will show that great minds sometimes think alike, even in literary endeavour, and that perhaps Stoker owed more than is acknowledged to Le Fanu.

Joseph Thomas Sheridan Le Fanu was born on 28 August 1814 to Thomas Philip Le Fanu and Emma Lucretia Dobbin Le Fanu and the following year the family moved to Phoenix Park on the appointment of Thomas Philip as chaplain to the Royal

Hibernian Military School. They left the park in 1826 on the father's appointment as Dean of Emly, and moved to Abington, County Limerick; but Le Fanu was to use the park and his time there as inspiration and source for his later stories.

Creativity ran in the blood since Le Fanu's grandmother Alice Sheridan Le Fanu, and her brother, Richard Brinsley Sheridan, were both playwrights. The younger Le Fanu's work included short stories and novels concerning the strange and the supernatural.

Grown to manhood, Le Fanu studied law at Trinity College Dublin and passed the bar; but opted for journalism and a life as a writer rather than remain in the legal profession. Le Fanu edited Dublin University Magazine, which published many of his works in serial form under a pseudonym. Prospering, he bought three Dublin newspapers and amalgamated them as the daily Evening Mail which flourished for more than 100 years.

Le Fanu is sometimes said to be the father of the Victorian Irish ghost story. His *Ghost Stories of Chapelizod* were published in the *Dublin University Magazine* in 1851. *The House by the Churchyard* (1863) is also set in Chapelizod. The physical location of the fictional house is the subject of local discussion to this day. *The House by the Churchyard* was published in monthly instalments, beginning in 1861, in *Dublin University Magazine* under the pseudonym of its narrator Charles de Cresseron.

Le Fanu's short story "The Village Bully" had its principal action near to the Chapelizod turnstile where a commemorative plantation of trees now stand, and at the top of Knockmary Hill in the background. The park wall beside the graveyard also featured in the ghost story. The story describes how the Bully Larkin picked a fight with a simple chap called Long Ned Moran and in the ensuing fist fight at the top of the hill, within sight of the Hibernian Academy (where the young Le Fanu had lived), Moran was beaten to a pulp and died within the year.

Larkin became subdued following the incident and took up work in the Chief Secretary's garden. He walked home to Chapelizod each evening across the Fifteen Acres until one night, arriving late at the turnstile, he was startled to see the ghost of Long Ned climb the wall from the churchyard, where his body was buried, and approach him. The ghost touched the hand of the bully, who suffered a debilitating stroke that left him unable to work and reduced him to begging for alms for many years before he too died.

The Royal Irish Artillery was stationed in Chapelizod at this time and another of Le Fanu's stories concerns a column of marching ghosts passing through the town when an inebriated Peter (the narrator) is prevailed upon to accompany an officer to a house that looks out on the sloping parkland. The tale, "The Spectre Lovers", concerns the married officer's affair with a young local woman and the possibility that a child had died. The fate of its body remains a mystery at the end of the story, beyond allusion to a treasure buried beneath a stone beyond the window. The lovers' wail was "like a distant summer wind, in the dead hour of night, wandering through ruins," wrote Le Fanu.

The House by the Churchyard is also set in Chapelizod, but a century earlier. However, the action encompasses Phoenix Park as much as anywhere else. Indeed, a principal character, the military surgeon Sturk, is attacked in Butchers' Wood near Castleknock Gate in the park and left lying for dead, with two fractures of the skull, in a lonely nook with bird song all around. He is taken home to Chapelizod, but never recovers from his injuries.

Le Fanu shows his personal knowledge of Phoenix Park when he has the assailant travel from the Magazine Fort on St Thomas' Hill in the southeast corner to the western extremity to carry out the attack and to vanish at the water's edge of the Liffey to the south east. In real life, the area where the surgeon was attacked was notoriously unsafe for travellers.

The *Nation* Newspaper

In the same century, and following a different literary tradition of nationalism, the Irish revolutionary Thomas Davis in 1841 was walking in Phoenix Park with his college friend, John Blake Dillon, a barrister, when they met the young journalist Charles Gavan Duffy. Continuing on their walk, they conceived the idea of producing a newspaper to support their cause. Davis was a Protestant, the others were Catholics and with Duffy as editor they published *The Nation*, whose first weekly issue appeared on 15 October 1842. Its slogan was "Educate that you may be Free". It published much material from members of the Young Irelanders, the revolutionary group of the time.

Ireland's first Governor General, Tim Healy, who was to live in the Vice Regal Lodge, worked as a parliamentary correspondent for *The Nation* before becoming Member of Parliament for Wexford in 1880; he carried his journalistic shorthand skills with him into later life. The paper folded eventually and the title was appropriated by the ruling Fianna Fáil party in September 2003 for its party magazine.

Oliver St John Gogarty

The opening of James Joyce's *Ulysses* features "stately plump Buck Mulligan", a character based on Joyce's contemporary Oliver St John Gogarty who, unlike Joyce, remained in Ireland and played a part in forming modern Ireland. Gogarty served as a Senator in the first Senate of the Irish Free State. At the Paris Olympics of 1924, when Ireland made its first appearance in an Olympic Games as an independent nation, no medals in the sporting events were won by Ireland. However, Gogarty was awarded a bronze medal for his "Ode to the Tailteann Games" in the Literature division.

In his autobiography, *As I Was Going Down Sackville Street* (1937), Gogarty recalled how as a small boy he was present in the

Vice Regal Lodge at a buy-Irish promotion being conducted by the powers that be of the time. He was dressed as an "Irishman" — kitted out in knee breeches and top hat, and even carried a shillelagh. He was driven there but had to walk home when it was over. Once used, then discarded.

Years later, he arrived in his car to visit Governor General Tim Healy in the great house. While awaiting clearance to drive in, he observed that the vale of the Liffey appeared deeper than it actually is from the plateau of Phoenix Park. But, he noted, the Dublin mountains in the distance rolled smooth as a deep wave through silver mists, an observation not altogether surprising from a poet.

Once inside, Healy asked Gogarty to invite his friend W.B. Yeats, "The Sally Gardener" to Healy's box at the Spring Show. Healy had invited some senior officers of the Free State army and their wives, and needed to entertain them, he told Gogarty.

Healy's response to the Nobel Laureate W.B. Yeats, who had written to him seeking a meeting in the Lodge, was to say: "Come and see me whenever you like in the bee-loud glade."

It struck Gogarty that it was now easier to visit the Lodge than it had been under the old regime. He wondered if it meant the Lodge had come down or he had come up in the world. It seemed, he noted in his autobiography, that the answer was "Yes" each way.

JAMES JOYCE

As he did with much of Dublin, James Joyce made ample use of Phoenix Park as a setting in a number of his short stories, and also in *Ulysses* and *Finnegans Wake*. In Joyce's short story "A Painful Case", the character James Duffy read in the *Evening Mail* (Le Fanu's real-life newspaper) of the death of Duffy's female friend Emily Sinico. The married lady was said to have a fondness for drink and was struck by a train while attempting to cross the railway at Sydney Parade in south Dublin. Duffy had already broken with her and the story closes as he stands upon Magazine Hill gazing down at furtive lovers by the park wall before walking away to his home in Chapelizod.

Joyce had his own connection with Chapelizod through his father John Stanislaus Joyce, and when Duffy gazes down into the old distillery from his lodgings he is looking at the distillery in Chapelizod, known as the Phoenix Park Distillery, a business Joyce's father had invested in at one time.

Joyce prided himself on detail in his writing and one section in *Ulysses* concerns a real-life question on Phoenix Park in Westminster scheduled for answer on 16 June 1904 — the day on which all action occurs in *Ulysses*, the day on which Nora Barnacle, later to be his wife, and Joyce first walked out together. Councillor J.P. Nannetti, MP for College Green for the Irish Party, had tabled a question on Phoenix Park to be asked on 16 June 1904. Disagreement had arisen between Nannetti and the Chief Secretary's Office as to the ownership of Phoenix Park. Nannetti contended that it belonged to the citizens of Dublin, and the Chief Secretary insisted it was the property of the Crown. The Secretary said: "The statement that the Phoenix Park belongs to the citizens of Dublin is pure fiction: it is the property of the Crown." Nannetti's parliamentary question elicited the information that the number of enclosures and allotments given over to polo and cricket would not be increased despite requests for more such facilities. (And while it has no real literary bearing, park management did write to an athletic body that called itself the Irish Brigade to tell it that its members would have to walk to the Fifteen Acres if they wanted to play ball games. The Brigade had wanted to use the Nine Acres area where polo is played instead.)

Though Joyce left Ireland and Phoenix Park behind him, his final novel, *Finnegans Wake* (1939) is partly set in Chapelizod and Phoenix Park. The story concerns a hod carrier called Finnegan who falls from a scaffold and dies; at his wake, whiskey splashes on the corpse, and he rises up again alive, as often happens.

Humphrey Chimpden Earwicker (HCE) is a foreigner who has married an Irish wife, Anna Livia Plurabelle, and they run a public house in Chapelizod. Scandal concerning an incident in Phoenix Park threatens HCE. The book is not an easy read and draws on all sorts of influences. The last sentence is incomplete and is closed by the sentence that starts the book. Start and end again.

PERCY FRENCH AND QUEEN VIC

In an earlier time, Percy French relayed a supposed after-dinner speech given by Queen Victoria when she complained about the revolutionary activist Maud Gonne dressing in black to welcome her majesty to Ireland.

The Queen's speech was notable for being overheard and cut into lengths of poetry by Jamesy Murphy, Deputy Assistant Waiter at the Vice Regal Lodge, according to French. The nonsense poem finds every line concluding with the words "sez she".

The good Queen even took a swipe at Willie Yeats for castigating her majesty in a letter to *The Irish Times* when he should be at home "French-polishing" his poems, according to French.

PATRICK KAVANAGH

Another Irish poet who did not know his place was Patrick Kavanagh who earned himself the distinction of being barred from Áras an Uachtaráin, for conduct unbecoming.

At a Red Cross reception on 24 July 1943 Kavanagh was invited with other journalists to the President's reception. Kavanagh was then a freelance journalist writing for the *Irish Press* as Piers Plowman. The journalists were issued with access-all-areas passes to allow them pursue their calling. However, Kavanagh stayed with the invited guests in the President's drawing room and accompanied them out to the garden for the presentation of a trophy.

An official report said Kavanagh generally behaved as if he was an invited guest, rather than a professional observer and representative of the press. The report stated, "His presence and his appearance were the subject of a considerable amount of comment. Under his coat he wore a green woollen jumper, and on his feet he wore sandals without socks, and generally looked untidy and not altogether clean." As a result, the decision was taken to ban him from future invitation. The memo said Kavanagh tended to be truculent with ministers, as well.

SEAMUS HEANEY

However, poets seemed to have mellowed by the time Seamus Heaney became Ireland's fourth Nobel Laureate for Literature in 1995. President Mary Robinson held a reception at Áras an Uachtaráin for the Heaney family when Heaney returned to Ireland.

Speaking on radio about his win, Heaney said, "I hope to go lightsomely with it." Lightsomely or not, a poem, "Beacons at

Seamus Heaney: "Beacons" at Farmleigh

Bealtaine" specially written by Heaney who was by then Ireland's de facto Poet Laureate, was read by him in Farmleigh House to the twenty-five Heads of State of the enlarged EU gathered there on May Day 2004 under Ireland's six-month presidency of the EU. The poem is placed on display in the Nobel Room at Farmleigh House.

On Accession Day, Heaney said: "There are those who say that the name Phoenix Park is derived from the Irish words, *fionn uisce*, meaning 'clear water' and that coincidence of language gave me the idea for this poem. It's what the poet Horace might have called a *carmen sæculare*, a poem to salute and celebrate an historic turn in the *sæculum*, the age."

Beacons at Bealtaine

Phoenix Park, May Day, 2004

Uisce: water. And *fionn*: the water's clear.
But dip and find this Gaelic water Greek:
A phoenix flames upon fionn uisce here.
Strangers were barbaroi to the Greek ear.
Now let the heirs of all who could not speak
The language, whose ba-babbling was unclear,
Come with their gift of tongues past each frontier
And find the answering voices that they seek
As fionn and uisce answer phoenix here.
The May Day hills were burning, far and near,
When our land's first footers beached boats in the creek
In uisce, fionn, strange words that soon grew clear;
So on a day when newcomers appear
Let it be a homecoming and let us speak
The unstrange word, as it behoves us here,
Move lips, move minds and make new meanings flare
Like ancient beacons signalling, peak to peak,
From middle sea to north sea, shining clear
As phoenix flame upon fionn uisce here.

TREES AND WRITERS

If trees are cut down to produce paper, Phoenix Park is doing its part in planting trees in honour of writers past.

In 2004, during the centenary celebrations for James Joyce's *Ulysses*, trees were planted in his memory near to the Wellington Monument. The centenary celebrations were to honour the day when the action of the fictional story occurred in Dublin, 16 June 1904.

A year earlier, in 2003, some trees were planted in commemoration of Sheridan Le Fanu just inside the Chapelizod turnstile. The small grove was planted by local residents Tomas Mac Giolla, the former Dublin Lord Mayor, and John Martin, chairman of Chapelizod Residents' Association. Parks Superintendent John A. McCullen facilitated the planting.

At least Le Fanu lived in the park for some of his life. A plantation of ninety-three trees, one for every year of his life, was planted for George Bernard Shaw, who neither lived in the park nor set any literary work there. The planting was launched by Minister of State Noel Tracey TD on 6 March 1992, to commemorate GBS. The plantation stands to the south of Chesterfield Avenue. The funds for the Shaw Plantation were raised by Mary Caulfield on behalf of the Dublin Shaw Society, according to a plaque at the site.

While not a literary link, a poignant event occured when local man Paddy Donnelly planted a single silver birch tree to commemorate the late Dr Alison O'Byrne, a young doctor who gave hope and encouragement to him through his cancer; ultimately it was he who planted the tree in her memory, when she pre-deceased him.

OTHER LITERARY ASSOCIATIONS

The Phoenix Park Distillery ceased production shortly after the new State was born; but stocks remained in bond for years afterwards and were checked by Maurice Walsh, yet another famous writer.

Walsh, author of "The Quiet Man" and other popular twentieth-century short stories and novels, lived in nearby Inchicore and worked in Chapelizod as the Excise Officer in the Phoenix Park Distillery. Walsh had opted to transfer from the customs service in Scotland to the new Free State following the treaty. The film of *The Quiet Man* was directed by John Huston in County Mayo and starred John Wayne and Maureen O'Hara. It remains hugely popular to this day, showing up regularly on television.

However, a 1953 twenty-three-minute two-reel film shot on location in Phoenix Park appears less often. That film followed the horror tradition laid down by Le Fanu when a young driver, played by Orson Welles, picks up a hitchhiker in the park with a strange tale to tell. The film, *Return to Glennascaul*, was nominated in 1953 for an Academy Award in the Best Two-Reel Short Subject category. It was produced by Louis Elliman and Micheál MacLiammóir. Hilton Edwards wrote and directed the black-and-white film.

A recent and more serious event in the park, Malcolm McArthur's dreadful murder of nurse Bridie Gargan in 1982, may have been the seed for *The Book of Evidence*, a novel by John Banville. The first-person account of an unhinged brute has clear parallels with the Phoenix Park murder of Nurse Gargan. The book was shortlisted for the Booker Prize, and won the Guinness Peat Aviation Award in 1989.

In 2005, local writer Christine Dwyer Hickey was shortlisted for the UK-based Orange Prize for Fiction for her novel *Tatty*, in which a little girl attends a boarding school that overlooks the park. Tatty and her father attend the Phoenix Park Racecourse through the stories. Dwyer Hickey's earlier work included a trilogy, *The Dancer, The Gambler* and *The Gatemaker*, and each had a scene set in the park. "Nearly everything that I have done has something about Phoenix Park in it. The very first success I had as a writer was a story called 'Across the Excellent Grass', which won at Listowel Writers Week 1992 and it was about a little girl going to the Phoenix Park races with her Dad," said Dwyer Hickey, who is now working on a collection of short stories to be entitled *Park Stories*, all of which will be set in Phoenix Park.

Phoenix Park's power to enthral and inspire has lost none of its potency over the centuries as successive generations of writers took pen in hand to record the real and imagined stories of Phoenix Park; and who is to say what is reality and what is fiction as shadows creep across the grass when daylight fades in the park?

7

MASS EVENTS

Phoenix Park is an area of contrasts. There is space for active recreation, and space for simply allowing solitude to ease away the cares of life. But on a few special occasions, the park has been host to large congregations of people gathered together for common purpose.

In former centuries, the greatest draw for the general populace were the frequent displays of military prowess held in the park. These would bring out an enthusiastic gathering, often accompanied by all sorts of merchants and hawkers — many of them there to slake the thirst of the crowd.

Following the decline of the appeal of noisy military bands and whiskey tents of earlier times, religious ceremony, motor races and pop concerts have been the biggest attractions for crowds in Phoenix Park. Indeed, the pop concert has taken over from religious observance as the draw for the masses in the twenty-first century.

The now misnamed Fifteen Acres is a flat expanse of some 200 acres of grassland at the centre of Phoenix Park, well suited to absorb large amounts of people, with room to spare. The largest number of people yet recorded on the Fifteen Acres was in September 1979 when an estimated one-third of the Irish population attended a mass celebrated by Pope John Paul II on an altar beneath where the Papal Cross now towers above all.

MILITARY REVIEWS, FENIANS AND PIONEERS

Reflecting changes wrought over the centuries, in the park and in the wider world, the open space was witness to different and more militant gatherings in earlier times. In 1780, two hundred years before the papal mass was celebrated, some 100,000 people attended to see the Irish Volunteers (Province of Leinster) review under their flag of "Loyal and Determined".

In the nineteenth century, when militarism was a way of life for many of Dublin's population, military reviews were watched by tens of thousands of people there on a day out to see brightly coloured uniforms and well-turned-out military formations complete with regimental bands, charging cavalry and loud huzzahs. The manoeuvres served the dual purpose of display and training for the bloody business of warfare in other parts of the British Empire.

In the Grand Review of 1844 some 5,000 men of the garrison of Dublin took part in exercises on the Fifteen Acres. The infantry formed an echelon of squares for a simulated attack on enemy cavalry, with the artillery being in action on the left and right. Thousands of citizens turned out to view the spectacle, according to contemporary reports. The British squares formation had played a decisive defensive role in the defeat at Waterloo of the French Emperor Napoleon by Wellington in 1815 some twenty-nine years earlier.

Not everybody, however, appreciated displays of armed prowess by the British army, and armed insurrections seeking Irish independence occurred every few generations throughout Ireland. A few decades after the Grand Review had taken place, the park's Nine Acres, off Chesterfield Avenue, where the modern polo grounds are situated, witnessed a police baton charge against some 5,000 people attending an August 1871 Fenian amnesty meeting. The organisers were attempting to pressure the Government to release prisoners, arrested during a failed 1867 Fenian uprising, when the police charged them. The ensuing furore in the Westminster parliament over police methods forced recognition of the right to hold public meetings without attack by the police.

The day chosen for the protest had coincided with a visit by the Prince of Wales and members of the royal family, who were staying at the Vice Regal Lodge, just up the road from the protest meeting place — a coincidence not unconsidered by the organisers of the assembly. Days before, the Under Secretary had issued notices forbidding the meeting, with unfortunate consequences for the battered protestors who had turned up for the meeting in any case — many of them giving as good as they got from the baton-wielding police.

However, the police seemed unconcerned when four years later, in May 1875, some 7,000 people gathered in the amphitheatre of the Hollow nearby to pass a resolution on behalf of the Dublin Total Abstinence League, condemning the sale of alcohol. The meeting had grown from the aspirations of the Irish Sunday Closing Association which was attempting to ban the consumption of alcohol on Sundays, a laudable if ultimately futile aspiration. In Phoenix Park on a Sunday at that time, up to 300 tents could be pitched on the Fifteen Acres for the sale of whiskey and for gambling.

Such shenanigans seemed to have gone on for some time, because under the care of Sir John Blaquiere, the Park Bailiff in the 1780s, the park was reportedly the scene of orgies almost approaching those of Donnybrook Fair in excess. In addition to drunken debauchery, the grasslands were overgrazed, and the roads left unrepaired. Not surprisingly, Blaquiere was eventually bought out of the job by the government of the day.

The Phoenix Park by-laws of 1926, under which the park is presently governed, now forbid the sale of any commodity in

Phoenix Park, including alcohol, unless under licence from the Commissioners of Public Works.

Meanwhile, demands for national agrarian reform saw a National Land League demonstration take place in 1880 when some 30,000 people assembled on the Nine Acres, off Chesterfield Avenue, to hear Michael Davitt speak on the subject. A year earlier, Davitt had founded the Land League, with Charles Stewart Parnell as president, to press their case.

CATHOLIC EMANCIPATION CENTENARY

The early twentieth century saw thousands of people travel from all parts of Ireland to be present at a Pontifical High Mass presided over by the Archbishop of Dublin, Most Rev Dr Byrne on Sunday, 23 June 1929, to mark the centenary of Catholic Emancipation in Ireland. Catholics had suffered greatly for some 150 years under the Penal Laws of the eighteenth and nineteenth centuries, which saw them oppressed and their rights denied, and a tithe levy imposed to pay for the upkeep of local ministers not of their own religious persuasion. However, emancipation was achieved under Daniel O'Connell's leadership in 1829. A hundred years later, in 1929, celebrations were held to commemorate the centenary of that emancipation, including the mass celebrated in Phoenix Park.

THE EUCHARISTIC CONGRESS

The next biggest religious function was the thirty-first Eucharistic Congress, held on 23 June 1932, just three years later. Preparations were in train for several months before the big occasion and the month of June became a period of retreat and prayer.

On the day, almost half a million people were present to witness Papal Legate Cardinal Lorenzo Lauri celebrate mass. Also present were high church dignitaries including nine cardinals, hundreds of bishops and other clerics representing forty-eight countries. During the High Mass, the 1,500-year-old St Patrick's Bell was used to mark the solemn moments. The bell was loaned for the occasion by the National Museum of Ireland. Scouts from the newly formed Catholic Boy Scouts of Ireland acted as guards at the high altar in the park. The High Mass was followed by a procession to the centre of the city along the North Circular Road and down O'Connell Street, where, at an altar erected on O'Connell Bridge, solemn benediction was imparted by Cardinal Lauri. The procession to the bridge was some five miles long and was given colour by the hundreds of banners carried by participants who wore the special Congress badge struck for the occasion.

The main gates at Parkgate Street were removed for ease of movement of crowds for the Eucharistic Congress and the gates went missing thereafter. The piers were later discovered to be nearby and were replaced in the later part of the twentieth century, but of the gates there was no word, until one turned up in County Cavan hanging as a gate on a private residence in the 1990s. Drawings and measurements were taken from this gate for future reference in the park. However, though the piers are restored, such is the width of modern coaches accessing the park that the original gate dimensions would not have allowed for the passage of such vehicles without damage.

An Tóstal and Dublin's Millennium

In 1953, Phoenix Park functioned as part of An Tóstal, a short-lived national initiative to create a three-week-long annual festival in the weeks following Easter that would see emigrants of Irish origin being welcomed home. The rump of the festival survives nowadays in Drumshanbo, County Leitrim, where An Tóstal festival is held every June.

While the national festival lasted in the 1950s, fireworks displays were held in the dark evening of Phoenix Park and were well attended in an era when fireworks were banned in general because they were munitions of a sort and it was thought by the national authorities that they should be kept out of the hands of the wrong people.

Dublin city millennium celebrations in 1988 saw several fireworks displays being offered to the citizens free of charge in the park. Even the EU joined in with free pyrotechnics for the citizenry. The serving Lord Mayor, Councillor Carmencita Hederman, graced the occasion with her presence, as did other city councillors who arrived for the occasion on a double-deck bus specially hired for their trip to the park.

VISIT OF POPE JOHN PAUL II

Few national events etched themselves in the memory of a generation as did the visit of Pope John Paul II to Ireland in 1979 in the early years of his twenty-seven-year-long papacy. On the Saturday morning, 29 September, an estimated million and a quarter people awaited the Pope's arrival on the Fifteen Acres. One third of the population of the entire country was on the Fifteen Acres on that day, an event unique by any standard.

While some 600,000 mass-goers arrived by bus and train from various parts of the country, many Dublin parishes simply walked in procession from their home areas to arrive at scheduled times in the park. From the air, the roads of the surrounding landscape were dense with lines of marching people all with the same destination: Phoenix Park.

Pedestrian gates to the park were locked and road gates were removed from most of the entrances — at Islandbridge, Chapelizod, White's Gate, Castleknock, Ashtown, Cabra and North Circular Road — to allow ease of access by the crowds of people wishing

A section of the vast crowd attending the papal mass in Phoenix Park

to attend the ceremony. The gates on the Back Road opposite the military cemetery on Blackhorse Avenue outside the park were not only removed but part of the wall was taken down temporarily for ease of movement. Stewards issued numbers to all visitors and a count was kept of people entering the park. In the event, the percentages of people entering were listed as follows, reflecting perhaps the distribution of housing in 1979, which was to change radically in the following years: Parkgate, 24 per cent; Islandbridge, 18 per cent; North Circular Road, 16 per cent; Blackhorse Avenue (Cabra), 14 per cent; Chapelizod, 10 per cent; Ashtown, 8 per cent; Castleknock, 6 per cent; and Knockmaroon, 2 per cent.

The organisers had asked those attending to bring their own seating. Manufacturers and retailers responded by selling lightweight folding picnic chairs of aluminium and nylon to the faithful at £2 each. When the day was done they picked up the seats and departed once more with the minimum of fuss and incident. The unrehearsed movement of such vast crowds with the guidance of some 12,000 volunteer stewards without incident was a marvel in itself. Some 600 gardaí were on duty for the visit, but the entire event was trouble-free.

Plans were made to accommodate some 3,000 mentally handicapped people, 1,500 deaf people, 1,500 blind people, 1,268 VIPs of one description or another and 4,156 clerics, not to mention 600 members of the press who were dispatched to record it all. Those accommodated at the front of the crowds were provided with long benches to sit on and to pray from.

The deer herd had been moved away from its usual haunt of Fifteen Acres and the great flat area was divided off into blue-roped corrals with wide corridors separating them, for safety. These crowd corrals stretched across the flat plain of Fifteen Acres. Each roped corral held 1,000 people and forty miles of rope were used to enclose the corrals. The arriving crowds were simply directed, with their individual folding seats, into the enclosures by volunteer stewards. When one corral was full, the next was opened and so it went until almost all of the more than 200-acre space was filled with people come to hear and see the first Pope to visit Ireland. Some 1,500 toilet cubicles were provided, as were 5.6 kilometres of ringwater mains, installed by Dublin Corporation.

Warm autumn winds had ripped asunder half of the sixty huge papal banners running along the rear boundary on the day before the papal mass. Dozens of seamstresses worked together to repair the damage before the Pope arrived, and Irish Naval Service personnel replaced the banners on the flag poles in time for the ceremonies.

With just eight weeks' notice of the impending visit of the Pope, the Dublin firm of Scott Tallon Walker architects had been awarded the design and project co-ordination contract. The altar had been erected twelve metres above the ground on a stepped and carpeted timber platform of an acre in size. The success of the Irish visit led to the firm being engaged as consultants for subsequent papal visits to other countries.

At 11.00 am, Pope John Paul II's plane, St Patrick, a Boeing 747 in the livery of Aer Lingus, passed over Phoenix Park. While the plane with its Irish military escort flew high across the Fifteen Acres, on the approach to Dublin Airport, the crowd waved flags and cheered. Bishop John Magee, who was the Pope's personal secretary at the time and who was on the flight, later said the Pontiff left his seat to bless the people below as the aircraft flew over the park. The flight landed shortly afterwards at Dublin Airport and the Pope was helicoptered to the park to celebrate mass and to meet the largest congregation of Irish people ever gathered in one place.

Tenor Frank Patterson sang "Panis Angelicus", and mezzo soprano Bernadette Greevy sang the "Magnificat" (as she was to do some twenty-six years later in a sunset ceremony held on the same spot to mark the Pope's passing in 2005). A 5,000-strong choir was accommodated beside the altar.

The hierarchy had asked the faithful to attend confession in preparation for receiving communion at the papal mass. In his homily, Pope John Paul II said news of so many people attending confession had given him great joy: "If there is someone who is still hesitating, for one reason or another, please remember this: the person who knows how to acknowledge the truth of guilt, and asks Christ for forgiveness, enhances his own human dignity and manifest spiritual greatness." Some forty potters had made 2,000 communion bowls in anticipation and more than 2,000 ministers of the Eucharist distributed Holy Communion during the mass.

During his homily, the Pope spoke of materialism and the threat to belief by new challenges relayed to the Irish as never before by new means of communication: "Like Saint Patrick, I too have heard the voice of the Irish calling to me. And so I have come to you, to all of you in Ireland."

Hundreds of priests kneel before tables holding 2,000 communion bowls, for distributing the Eucharist to the crowds at the papal mass

So vast was the crowds and the distance from the altar so great for some that the Pope's words were carried on the public address system long before the rolling applause of those at the front reached those at the back of the congregation.

The Polish Pope said he was living a moment of intense emotion standing in the company of so many hundreds of thousands of Irish people in Phoenix Park. He recalled the missionaries the Irish had sent to other countries, including his native Poland, to preach the gospel. He recalled how many times the Eucharist had been celebrated in Ireland, from medieval and modern cathedrals, to nineteenth-century mass rocks in the glens and forests when Catholics were penalised for practising their religion. He said the gathering was at one with the vast throng which filled Phoenix Park on the occasion of the Eucharistic Congress in 1932.

The crowd at the Eucharistic Congress in 1932 had included twenty-two-year-old Kathleen Connolly from the Liberties who had paid a hard-earned and expensive half a crown to buy a small brown attaché case in which to pack sandwiches and a bottle of cold tea for the High Mass in the park. Half a million people sat on short brown wooden forms on the Fifteen Acres to hear papal count John McCormack sing "Panis Angelicus" at the Pontifical High Mass. Kathleen and thousands of others later followed happily after the fluttering banners to benediction on O'Connell Bridge in the city.

In 1979, Kathleen, by now a sixty-nine-year-old grandmother, and her growing family, were amongst the million and more who walked back into the park in September to welcome the Pope to their city and home.

Many who attended the Pope's mass brought home their adhesive corral passes as a memento of that highly emotional day. The day was made all the more memorable when Pope John Paul II, ever the showman, mounted a specially built "Popemobile" on the back of a D-series Ford truck, and travelled at walking pace through the corridors between the corrals, so that almost every one of the

The pope greets the congregation at the papal mass

million and a quarter people got a close-up view of the Pope at some point as he waved and smiled. Having completed his traverse of the park, the Pope returned to the helicopter for lift-off to Drogheda and ceremonies there.

Behind, he left an emotional crowd and lifelong memories that would be recalled whenever the thirty-five-metre-high Papal Cross was contemplated. Over a quarter of a century later, the steel cross still stands in Phoenix Park as a place of private pilgrimage for many. Much smaller commemorative crosses that were left standing at the other two great Catholic gatherings in the park, the Eucharistic Congress and the centenary celebrations for Catholic Emancipation, went missing afterwards, removed by persons unknown.

It was originally planned to leave the forty-tonne steel cross in place for just ten weeks after the visit. Instead, following representations to the OPW, it became a permanent feature of the park and the accompanying backstage service area car park became a rendezvous point for many visitors, not to mention serving as a starting point for much of the park-based activity enjoyed by many groups of various interests. For example, the car park, at certain times, serves at night as a gathering point for amateur astronomers intent on studying the heavens for movement.

In the aftermath of the 1979 Papal visit, the mound below the cross had been considered for an indoor display and memorial of the occasion; but subsequent development of the Visitor Centre in the grounds of the old Papal Nunciature saw it being moved there instead. The Nunciature, situated at Ashtown Castle, had under British rule been the residence of the Under Secretary for Ireland. In accordance with Vatican custom, the Nunciature, like all others throughout the world, had a throne room reserved for the reigning Pope, in the event of his visiting Ireland. As it happened, the Nunciature in the park closed down a year earlier in 1978 and Pope John Paul II instead stayed in the new residence in Cabra when he visited Dublin.

The Papal Cross under construction in 1979

Communion bowls and other artefacts from the papal visit are on permanent display in the Visitor Centre, as are photographs of the large crowds and of the ceremonies on the day.

MEMORIAL SERVICE FOR POPE JOHN PAUL II

The papal visit was the last occasion when crowds of any size turned out for a religious ceremony in Phoenix Park. The gathering on the death of the same Pope some twenty-six years later was a more subdued and smaller affair.

On that chilly evening, 8 April 2005, fewer than 10,000 people gathered at a funeral mass for the late Pontiff who had died in Rome on 2 April aged eighty-four, after a lingering illness. Taoiseach Bertie Ahern TD and several government ministers were among the crowd.

The wide leather-covered wooden seat used by the Pope more than a quarter of a century earlier was brought from its permanent display in the Phoenix Park Visitor Centre and placed unoccupied on an altar specially erected under canvas at the top of the mound where the Pope had celebrated mass on that temperate autumn day in what was by then the previous century.

The Papal Nuncio to Ireland, Most Rev Dr Guiseppe Lazzarotto represented the Vatican at the concelebrated mass. Rev Eamonn Walsh, Auxiliary Bishop of Dublin, in his address urged those present to help bring people back to the Catholic Church. Music was provided by the Army Number 1 Band and by the Dublin Diocesan Music Group, as footage of the Pontiff's Irish visit was shown on three giant TV screens.

The disappointing turnout was in marked contrast both to the 1979 visit and to the huge crowds who had travelled to Rome for the late Pope's funeral. The organisers had believed some 30,000 people would attend the sunset service of remembrance, and the Office of Public Works prepared crowd control and stewarding for up to 100,000 people, just in case. A huge public address system was put in place. Miles of steel barriers snaked around the open and empty acres. The deer herd was again moved to a safe place around the Ordnance Survey Office. Once more, the park was closed to motor traffic until 10.00 pm on the day and during the afternoon Dublin Bus provided a free service from the city centre for those wishing to attend the ceremony.

But a biting cold dry easterly wind and live broadcasts of the actual funeral earlier in the day from Rome did not encourage large crowds to attend the 6.30 pm mass on a working Friday. Many who gathered earlier in the April afternoon brought bouquets of flowers to add to those already in place on the grass bank sloping away from the papal cross.

Members of Ireland's by now numerous Polish population attended and flew their and the late Pope's national flag. Hawkers sold holy candles for €1 or €2 each; many people lit them with a prayer and left them below the Papal cross.

However, as the weekend followed, many made private pilgrimages to the park and the mound of flowers grew larger as a red and white Polish flag flanked a black flag on either side of the floral tribute to the departed pontiff, as his empty chair was returned to the Visitor Centre across the road.

SOCCER FEVER

In 1994, celebration of another kind was offered to the Irish soccer team under Jack Charlton's management when they were welcomed home on the Fifteen Acres from the World Cup by hundreds of thousands of people. Before they arrived on the reviewing stand, the team was welcomed to Áras an Uachtaráin by President Mary Robinson, and it was difficult to believe in the blazing sunshine that the team had in fact been knocked out of the tournament, such was the warm enthusiasm shown by the crowds for their heroes.

The homecoming was accompanied by musical performances and is notable for the early appearance of the nascent boy band Boyzone, performing in bright orange boiler suits in brilliant sunshine, before they went on to achieve worldwide fame.

On 18 June 2002, the World Cup national soccer team, by now under manager Mick McCarthy, the former Captain Fantastic, also had a homecoming in Phoenix Park, this time in front of the park's soccer pavilions. More than 100,000 people massed on the soccer pitches to cheer the team. Once more, the team had been knocked out of the World Cup, this time on penalties, but the crowds were just happy that they were there at all, and cheered mightily when the players landed on the stage. The crowd sang "Happy Birthday" to Jason McAteer, roared when Packie Bonner took a bow, and cheered just as proudly when a number of English accents declared emotionally that they were proud to be Irish.

Mick McCarthy told the holders of a banner saying they were "Mick McCarthy's Baby" that they could not come home to his house to be fed: "There's too many of ye." It was all good fun and free entertainment for all concerned.

MUSIC IN THE PARK

Music has always played a role in the life of Phoenix Park, from the trumpeters accompanying the military reviews of centuries past, right up to the concerts — pop, rock, classical and traditional — now held frequently in the summertime.

In the early years of the twentieth century, the Dublin United Tramways Company sponsored the services of brass bands and paid them about £4 per performance for performing on the bandstand in the Hollow, beside the Zoo. The tramway company had a fleet of trams waiting at Parkgate Street to convey people to various parts of the city. A band in the park brought good business to the company as well as providing free entertainment for thousands of Dubliners.

For many Dubliners, the concerts were a meeting place when, from 4.00 to 6.00 on Sunday afternoons they joined in popular choruses to musical accompaniment. Later, the bands would parade as far as Parkgate Street and the awaiting trams, in a neat and musical display of opportune and constructive marketing.

The practice of public performances ended with the beginning of the First World War, when most bands and band members were called to other duties.

Park management revived the summer Sunday afternoon free concerts in the 1990s and they continue to this day. However, the emphasis has moved from military-type bands to a more country and folk programme, although brass and reed bands are still a popular draw.

No matter how popular the weekly performances are, they pale when compared to the huge crowds that attend the pop concerts that have been allowed in the park since 2002 when it was decided that five large-scale events, which require road closures, would be permitted in Phoenix Park each year. Under current regulations, the Commissioners licence a number of concerts through the year in the park with five such licences being available annually upon application and approval. One of these events was to be the motor races, so options are open for the remaining four availabilities. The practice has been for a free sponsored concert to be held during the summer, with a paid ticket concert being promoted on another occasion.

While concerts are now held within the park walls, the closest some concertgoers in 1983 got to the U2 gig on 14 August was sleeping out in the park the night before the Sunday show kicked off on the old Phoenix Park Racecourse. The concert was promoted by Radio 2 as RTÉ's 2FM was known then. "A Day at the Races" was billed as "U2 and Friends". The friends included Simple Minds, Eurythmics, Big Country, Steel Pulse and Perfect Crime. Bono even brought his own dad on to the stage for a swift appearance. The attendance is recorded at 20,000 people, though some say there were 25,000 there, while others report that a fence was torn down and some more heads poured into the show for free. The ticket price was £10.50 in advance or £12 on the day.

It was a day of high excitement. It was the Edge's birthday and the crowd sang "Happy Birthday" to him. And the announcement from the stage that Eamon Coughlan had just won the 5,000-metre race in a time of 13 minutes 18.53 seconds from Werner Schildhauer in the World Championships in Helsinki added to bonhomie of the Irish. Coughlan used the park over the years as a home training ground through the local Donore Harriers Club.

Some nineteen years later, on 18 August 2002, the first free pop concert took place heralding a new era of music in Phoenix Park itself. The venue was the Whitefields part of the park, and not on the Fifteen Acres, as at first envisaged. Sponsored by O2 Ireland, the mobile phone company, in association with 2FM, attendance was restricted to 100,000 people. However, since the park itself was not closed to public access, the show was heard beyond the concert site by people who did not get tickets. Some thirty acts appeared on stage between noon and 8.00 pm. Many acts sang just one or two songs, and excitement waned more than it waxed for most of the afternoon. English pin-up singer Darius was presented with a huge cake by popstars Six and boyband Reel as thousands of children sang "Happy Birthday" to him and anybody else who had a birthday around that time. Also making appearances were Bellefire, Samantha Mumba, Omero Mumba, Lulu and Ronan Keating.

It was very much a day for the teens and preteens. No alcohol sellers were allowed into the grounds and the biggest problem faced by the St John's Ambulance volunteers on the day was people reporting in with headaches. The Garda found and reunited people by simply telling all officers by radio just who was awaiting collection in their reunification tent.

The leakage of concert-goers turned into a flood after former Boyzone member Ronan Keating ended his four-song act at about 6.00 pm and thousands of people descended on waiting shuttle buses to go back to the city. Unusually, the buses waited on Chesterfield Avenue for their mostly young passengers.

A Robbie Williams show on 9 August 2002 was the first commercial concert to be allowed in the public park. More than 500 gardaí and a drug unit patrolled the open-air pop concert, with some 135,000 ticket-buyers in attendance. Gates opened at 1.00 pm and warm-up acts performed from 3.00 pm with Williams on stage at 8.30 pm for a two-hour set.

By 2005, among those performing at the free concert were choirgirl-turned-pop-diva Charlotte Church, the Saw Doctors, Derry city's Claire Sprule, and the Camembert Quartet, amongst others. The free park concert, unlike most concerts, has no age restriction. However, people left the concert site in significant numbers throughout the afternoon, with some explaining that children in their care were tired or, worse still, "bored".

As Dublin has grown and spread past Phoenix Park, so too has usage of the park increased in recent years. More people can be seen in the landscape at the formerly quieter western end of the park, for instance. And with five major road-closing events allowed for in a year, more and more people will choose to have the Phoenix Park experience, alone or with massed crowds of like-minded individuals.

8

SPORTS AND RECREATION

The rolling grasslands and clear roads of Phoenix Park have long been a draw for sports and sportspeople alike. From motor racing and cycling, to polo, cricket, soccer and hurling, the wide expanses allow for a broad range of activities.

Phoenix Park lends itself to team and individual sports and to non-competitive sporting pastimes alike. Occasional objections from some quarters to partial closures merely reflect competing demands for space in the park.

Indeed, management plans for the park include optimum usage of playing pitches and facilities, which means making the maximum use of available resources compatible with maintenance of the pitches, without deterioration. Park by-laws state: "No person shall take part in the game of polo, cricket, football, or other game the playing of which in the Park is not contrary to these by-laws, save in such places in the Park as the Commissioners shall set apart for the playing thereof respectively, and subject to and in accordance with such directions (if any) as may be given by a park constable or by the Superintendent or Assistant Superintendent of the Park." Within these restrictions, the park provides outstanding opportunities for both active and passive recreational pursuits.

However, the majority of soils in the park afford poor natural drainage and are therefore unsuitable for playing fields. As a result, upkeep of the playing pitches requires the monitoring of

As this photograph (taken around 1940) of Chesterfield Avenue shows, Phoenix Park has long been a draw for a variety of activities, with camogie players, walkers, cyclists and drivers all sharing the space (© National Library of Ireland, Eason Collection 1699)

pitch conditions in adverse weather and the systematic control of pitch usage.

Nonetheless, management objectives for use of the park in general include encouragement of appropriate recreational use. Any measures required to enable the park to contribute fully to the development of "Sport-for-All" policies are sympathetically considered, provided they are compatible with park management objectives. Recreational uses, in addition to codes that require a fixed playing field, are encouraged and include well-organised running and cycling events on park roads, jogging, walking and orienteering, and fitness training.

Within the intensive recreation zone, the playing pitches designated for use for Gaelic and soccer are managed in accordance with an optimum usage policy. In addition to the better known football and hurling sports, there are a number of long-standing uses of specific areas of the park by particular clubs for other sports. These include the Army athletic grounds, the Phoenix and Civil Service

Cricket Clubs, and the polo grounds. However, at least since 1886, there has been an official direction that space allocated for cricket and polo and other allotments in the park should not be increased.

WALKING, CYCLING, CROSS-COUNTRY AND ATHLETICS

The use of park roads for well-organised competitive running and cycling races and for charity walks and runs is encouraged.

The annual Dublin City Marathon, run on October bank holiday Monday, includes a section of the park in its circuit for runners and walkers, when the roadway is closed to vehicular traffic, for a change.

Earlier in the year, in June, the Dublin International Grand Prix of Race Walking takes place on a closed two-kilometre course on Furze Road. Contestants came in 2005 from some thirty-six countries to the park to participate in the strictly controlled speed-walking event. Some athletes take part in Dublin Grand Prix in the park as final preparation for competing in major championships elsewhere later in the year.

On the less competitive side, an annual Simon Community Fun Run takes place in late autumn. Organisers run it as a novelty event. The distance is five kilometres, well within walking comfort for the average healthy person. Celebrities turn out on the day and part of the fun is to see who has turned up in fancy dress. The route starts and ends at the Papal Cross and participants head west on Chesterfield Avenue, turn south at Mountjoy crossroads and skirt the Furry Glen and St Mary's Hospital to return to the finishing line. (See Walking in a Circle in Chapter 12.)

For health walkers, the Irish Heart Foundation has placed ten one-kilometre markers along the all-weather paths on Chesterfield Avenue. There are five markers on either side, but discounting the first one as the starting point reduces the distance to four kilometres in both directions, giving a total of eight kilometres for the entire

Slí na Sláinte route. The trail is just one of the way-marked walks developed by the Irish Heart Foundation to encourage people to walk for at least thirty minutes a day.

On Chesterfield Avenue, slí markers were designed to be compatible with existing park railings and bollards, which range from Victorian handrails made by the Kennan Foundry in Fishamble Street, where Handel's *Messiah* was first performed, to granite bollards and ordnance benchmarkers. The new uprights are low in height, have curved edges, and are made of black iron.

There is also a private slí, marked by signs of the standard woodland design used elsewhere in countryside settings, for staff and residents of Áras an Uachtaráin within the grounds of the Áras, which extends to three kilometres in length. (See also Chapter 12 for some other suggested walks in the park.)

Cars, walkers, runners and cyclists all have their day in the park; but where once the horse was the principal means of transport

The People's Flower Gardens have always been
a popular spot for the casual stroller

in traversing Phoenix Park, use of today's park by the non-polo-playing horse is restricted to approved bridle paths under licence, though mounted gardaí may also be seen on their charges on the way to and from the stables in Áras an Uachtaráin from their duties in the city.

Use of the park by recreational cyclists on the other hand is encouraged and in recent years major funds have been expended to facilitate commuting and fun cyclists travelling along Chesterfield Avenue. Three lines of lime beech and horse chestnut run on either side of the main road and date from the 1840s when park planner Decimus Burton decided that Chesterfield Avenue should be the grand avenue of Phoenix Park. A new path was laid in recent years between the straight lines of mature trees and the existing path beside the road was resurfaced and designated as a cycleway. Joggers, in turn, choose to run on a third path worn on the very inside of the trees where the ground has been pounded hard by countless running feet over the years. At any given time, there could be four streams of movement on either side of the main road: motor traffic, cyclists and rollerbladers, walkers and joggers all studiously ignoring one another as they roll along.

In the mid-1950s the park welcomed the Rás Tailteann, the Irish national cycle race, to its roads and it has been racing through the park ever since. Throughout the summer months, parts of the roads are closed to accommodate a series of cycle races. The Rás Tailteann is the longest-running sponsored event in Irish sport and celebrated its fiftieth anniversary in 2002. FBD Insurance took over sole sponsorship of the event in 2005 and renamed it as the "FBD Insurance Rás". The eight-day around the country race concludes with a fifty-kilometre speed circuit in Phoenix Park. As part of the elite international calendar, the race is eligible to award qualifying points required for participation in Olympic Games and World Cycling Championships. Requests for invitations to compete in the race come from racers in South Africa, Germany, France, Canada, Denmark, Moldova and other countries. Previous winners

The Tour de France took a diversion through Phoenix Park in July 1998

include Stephen Roche and Shay O'Hanlon. O'Hanlon dominated the domestic cycling scene in the 1960s and rode the Rás on twenty-two occasions. He was the first Irish rider to win a stage on the Tour de France and wear the coveted yellow jersey. Stephen Roche won the Tour de France in 1987. In July 1998 cyclists competing in the Tour de France visited the park on 12 July as part of its multi-staged journey to the finishing line in Paris.

More than 100 years earlier, in 1896, Dublin jeweller Samuel Waterhouse presented the newly formed Donore Harriers club with a shield for a ten-mile handicap cross-country race. Now known as The Waterhouse-Baird-Byrne Shield, the trophy has been competed for every year since then, except in 1916 when many runners were otherwise involved in the Great War. The Christmas race is now the oldest club cross-country event in the world. It attracts competitors to the park year after year in the mid-winter.

Indeed, club president and author Maurice Ahern recalled the determination of club member Davie Baird who, in 1916, joined the 10th Battalion of The Royal Dublin Fusiliers and was badly wounded at the Battle of Ancre in France. "Nonetheless, he fully recovered and went on to win the coveted prize in 1920, 1921 and for a third time in 1937. He also re-presented the trophy to the club," said Ahern.

Irish Olympian Eamon Coughlan, a member of the Chapelizod-based club, who became world 5,000-metre champion in 1983, recorded the fastest time ever for the ten-mile shield race when he became the only man to run under fifty minutes for the event in the park.

Donore Harriers is typical of sporting organisations that have made the park their home. Founded in 1893, the club, in 1948, moved into premises in Hospital Lane, Islandbridge, where it remained for some forty-two years while using the park for its outdoor activities. In 1990, a modern sports centre was built on

Two sports for the price of one: bicycle polo

the banks of the River Liffey at Chapelizod just 100 metres outside the Chapelizod Gates of the park. The club describes Phoenix Park as a wonderful facility for both the club and for Irish athletics.

POLO

The park's own countryside setting is underlined by the chuck of polo players striking the ball as polo ponies race around the nearby polo grounds, which have been in use since the 1870s. The polo season lasts from May to September and matches are played on weekend days at 3.00 pm. Spectators can watch the games free of charge each weekend and, while spectator attendance has diminished somewhat over the years, the games continue to have a loyal following.

The All-Ireland Polo Club was founded in 1873 by Horace Rochford, and the club has played on the Nine Acre field ever since. At the end of the nineteenth and the beginning of the twentieth

Polo in the Park

century, polo in the park attracted larger crowds in those pre-television days. In 1893, the reported attendance at one tournament was 15,000. In 1909, there were an estimated 30,000 watching the riders compete.

Railings were placed on the southern side of the ground and the ground was drained into the lake in the Zoo to create a better playing surface. However, the old Victorian pavilion was seriously damaged by fire in 1987 with the loss of historic photographs, paintings, sketches and club records. The following year, the club was reinstated to some of its former glory with a renovated clubhouse restored to its original Victorian design, complete with elegant railings and intricate woodwork.

CRICKET

Not far away from the polo grounds and across Chesterfield Avenue, the pavilion of Phoenix Cricket Club was also damaged, in this instance by a German bomb dropped on the park in May 1941, during the Second World War. Rocks fell through the clubhouse roof and the pitch was unplayable because of stones strewn across the surface. Curiously, the neighbouring Civil Service Cricket Club had its roof lifted off and re-settled back into its original position by the blast.

Cricket in the park, however, faced a problem of vandalism in the late nineteenth century. Few ordinary people had taken an interest in playing team games in an Ireland recovering from famine; just surviving was the priority for many. But as some prosperity and recovery followed, the bicycle came on the market — with unforeseen consequences for the state of cricket surfaces. The bike meant people with mischief in mind could travel farther to cause harm for others and the cricket pitches in the park suffered for some time from intrusions by bike-riding vandals.

Nicknamed "the mob" in general, many people of differing backgrounds began to play other games on the carefully tended cricket grounds. After being subjected to invigorating games of football, the cricket surface was well-nigh unplayable by cricketers. Since many of the vandals arrived on bikes, it followed that most, if not all, were well-to-do people and not members of the dispossessed classes who might have been thought to harbour ill-feeling towards the ruling classes and forces of occupation whose sport it was at the time.

In an echo of such past problems caused by improved mobility, steps were taken in late 2005 to close the car park at the Papal Cross at 9.00 pm each evening following the gathering there of boy racers in fast cars who then drove to race one another to various destinations outside of the park.

Phoenix Cricket Club, founded in 1830, was once one of eleven clubs that played in Phoenix Park, but now shares the cricket pitch area only with Civil Service Cricket Club. The Phoenix cricket ground is one of the oldest in unbroken use in the world. Phoenix is also the only cricket club in the park whose caretaker is allowed reside

Phoenix Cricket Club at play

156

in the pavilion. In any case, according to park regulations, licences granted to cricket clubs occupying enclosed ground provide for the playing of cricket or lawn tennis only.

The neighbouring Civil Service is the fourth oldest cricket club in Ireland after DUCC, Phoenix and Cork County, and as such is one of the country's longest-surviving sporting institutions. In the early 1860s, George Howard, Earl of Carlisle and also the serving Lord Lieutenant of Ireland, who had his own pitch laid out in the Vice Regal Lodge up the road, persuaded parliament no less to grant civil servants a cricket ground in Phoenix Park, right beside the Dog Pond, where the Civil Service Cricket Club play to this day. Howard, ever the keen cricketer, kept score when the club played its first match on the front lawn of the Vice Regal Lodge in April 1863, according to author and club historian Anthony Morrissey.

Morrissey also recorded the great difficulty in fielding a team on time on Saturdays, since civil servants worked a half-day on Saturday and were apt to be late in travelling from their place of work to the park: "Most if not all able-bodied civil servants were obliged to work on Saturday mornings . . . It was almost impossible for Civil Service to consistently field the best sides available."

The club subsequently built a wooden pavilion on its own ground with a bar in its basement, hardly a ball's throw from the Phoenix Cricket Club. This structure lasted for ninety years from 1879 before it was replaced. It was for a time one of the few places where drink could be had on Sunday night in Dublin, when many hostelries were closed under licensing laws. Card games took place there as well, though one such game was mercifully cancelled earlier on the night that the German bomb landed nearby. Of course, if late-night drinking was going on and a card game was in progress, the bomb may not have been noticed overmuch — after all, only the roof was raised!

Civil Service and Phoenix are separated by the lapping waters of the Dog Pond which on occasions has been the receptacle for many well-struck balls. Cricket and the park attracted visiting players including Charles Stewart Parnell, who brought a Wicklow side to play there in the 1870s.

The present membership of Civil Service Club includes players from Australia, India, Pakistan and South Africa, now living in Ireland, as well as players from the indigenous population.

There may even be a re-stirring of interest occurring in cricket in Phoenix Park. In its early days at the turn of the twentieth century, Bohemians FC fielded a cricket as well as a soccer team. The cricket team took its name from the medical school which a number of the founding players attended at the time. In 2005, it was announced that Bells Academy Cricket Club was being re-formed by a number of Bohemian FC fans.

Soccer

The western part of the Fifteen Acres is home to the soccer and Gaelic pitches known simply to many generations of Dubliners as "The Pitches".

Playing privileges are administered by park management. Teams in the mid-1900s had to pay two shillings to the ranger in charge for the use of the pavilion and that allocated pitch on the day. In return, he would issue two corner flags to the team. It was then an easy task to see which teams had paid their subs. No flag flying, no subs paid, and a discussion ensued with the ranger in charge. No fee, no game, and a red card. Off!

For more than forty years there was no electricity supply to the changing rooms and a water supply was in a trough, with two pipes feeding it. Very basic facilities apart, the sportspeople that used the pavilions were there for the game and for the love of sport and understood that as with everything in the park, change comes dropping slow. Some twenty-four changing rooms were finally refurbished in 2000. The pavilion building still has the same exterior today, to comply with heritage requirements, but the interior was

A soccer match on the park's pitches in the 1970s

transformed in the refurbishment. Electricity was provided for the first time, making it possible to have hot showers after a game, and drainage was improved.

The Leinster Junior League received a seventy per cent sports development grant of £400,000 to refurbish the complex. The playing pitches were upgraded and tubular steel was sunk into the ground to hold goalposts in lieu of slabs of grass-covered concrete that used to hold the posts. Athletes use the facilities at non-football times, and even film crews are sometimes accommodated there while filming goes on using the park as location.

The leading soccer club, Bohemian Football Club, is the oldest association football club in the Republic of Ireland. Founded in September 1890 at a meeting in the North Circular Road Gate Lodge of the park, Bohemians claim to be prime movers in re-establishing soccer in Dublin, the province of Leinster, and even further afield.

The first Bohemians played their football on the Polo Grounds, and each match day carried the goalposts to and from North Circular Road Lodge where they were stored. A plaque commemorating the founding of the Bohemian Football Club stands in the Lodge garden.

Interestingly, such storage of third-party goods was expressly forbidden under Regulation 16 of the 1919 Regulations to be observed by Gate Keepers of His Majesty's Phoenix Park, which stated that gatekeepers and constables are forbidden to take charge of bicycles or other property belonging to the public, or to allow same to be stored in a lodge or the enclosures connected therewith.

However, park constables even used the North Circular Road Lodge to store lost children at one time when the park was a popular destination for families on a day out! Rangers simply brought found children to the Lodge and directed lost parents to the same location until all were happily reunited and peace of a fashion was restored.

HURLING

Cricket was to lose much of its popular appeal in the years following the creation of the GAA. In 1882, the Dublin Hurling Club was formed by a group of men including one Michael Cusack, who later helped found the Gaelic Athletic Association, the GAA.

In a fraternal gesture, the All-Ireland Polo Club agreed to the use of their pitch for the new code. But the hurlers moved across the road after a while and used a pavilion of an older rugby club as headquarters.

The first hurling match planned for the Nine Acres had to be postponed because no manufacturer in Dublin knew how to make hurleys or sliotars (balls) for the game, since the skills had fallen into disuse. Balls and hurleys were produced some time later and the national game got underway at last.

Although this first club was to fail, the game enjoyed a resurgence following the official forming of the GAA in Thurles, County Tipperary on 1 November 1884.

After that, hurling sessions started up in earnest in Phoenix Park and continued each weekend on the grass near the Wellington Monument. Spectators by then were being encouraged to join in the games with many people consequently chasing a sliotar around the grass beneath the Iron Duke's stern memorial. Such enthusiastic participation in the game may account for the inclusion in Regulation 25 of the Regulations issued in 1919, and confirmed by the Free State in 1926, of an admonition to park constables to prevent ball games being played near the monument: "Use every endeavour to dissuade persons from playing football upon the open space around the Wellington Monument." The regulation probably covers hurling as well, since a belt from a sliotar is more noticeable than one from a football, however well-struck, and a herd of galloping hurlers will disrupt the most mannered of picnics.

TAKING TO THE AIR

However, the regulations say nothing at all about whether or not a helicopter is allowed to land on a playing field in the park — unsurprisingly, since there were no such things when the regulations were being drawn up!

The army athletic grounds are on the other side of the Dog Pond from the remaining cricket clubs. Its area is also used as a landing pad by helicopters from the air-sea rescue service when dropping patients from around the country for road transfer to Dublin hospitals.

But flying objects on a much smaller scale are a more common site in the park. Whether flying model aeroplanes and kites is a sport or an organised activity is a moot point for many aficionados. Model planes have been flying about Phoenix Park since the 1930s when early examples were free-flight models, with their tail fins fixed so as to fly in ever-widening circles as the plane climbed to the point when the fuel from the tiny engine was exhausted and the aircraft floated back down to earth once more towards the pursuing earthbound aviators.

Post-war, many enthusiasts took to control-line flying, and radio-controlled models made their appearance in due course. Indeed, the skies above the park were the cause of an air accident investigation of their own in 1998 when a home-designed model aircraft with a Titan 23cc spark ignition engine took off from the Fifteen Acres and landed at Dublin Airport. The errant plane was flying circuits at the registered aeromodel site on the Fifteen Acres. After a take-off, which followed a normal circuit, command was lost, according to an official air safety investigation report. The model then flew off in a north-east direction on its own. When its fuel was exhausted, the miniature plane glided to earth, and landed on the runway at Dublin Airport without much damage to the plane or the airport. The pilot of a Boeing B737, taxiing for take-off at Dublin Airport, observed the model aircraft parked on a link taxiway near the threshold of Runway 28. He reported its presence and airport security personnel removed it to the airport fire station. The subsequent report found the probable cause of loss of command was the exhaustion of the receiver battery.

While early model planes were circling the park during the 1930s, Phoenix Park's Fifteen Acres was being used as a landing strip for real planes when aerial displays were offered by pilots of light aircraft. Spectators were offered a trip in a plane out over Dublin Bay and back to the park for ten shillings a trip. The service ended when one pilot fatally crashed to earth while performing acrobatics over the landing strip. Before that sad accident, the planes had flown over what was once Phoenix Park's golf course.

GOLF

Scottish banker John Lumsden had pioneered the formation of the Royal Dublin Golf Club in 1885. The Dublin Golf Club, as it was first known, was based in Phoenix Park but as membership grew, a new home was sought and the club eventually moved to its present home on Bull Island at Clontarf in 1889.

In general, the course ran from a point near St Mary's Hospital and across the Fifteen Acres to a green near the back of what is now the American Ambassador's residence. The golfers then came back across towards Knockmary Hill and around by where the Cheshire Home now stands. They played along by the lower wall of the hospital to arrive once more on Fifteen Acres.

There is no golf course in the modern Phoenix Park. However, Dublin City Council developed a municipal course across the Liffey on lands at Ballyfermot that were once part of Phoenix Park and which are known to this day as the Phoenix Park Extension.

MOTOR RACING

Phoenix Park has had a long association with motor cars. While it may seem unlikely now, with commuter traffic congestion reaching a critical phase in the park, there was a time when cars travelling down the long straight of Chesterfield Avenue set world records for speed. In 1903, when the overall maximum speed limit on public roads had lately been raised from fourteen miles per hour to twenty miles per hour, a 70hp Mors car driven by the French Baron de Forest established a world record of 85.9 miles per hour during speed trials in the park.

The Phoenix Park Speed Trials were a part of Automobile Fortnight in Ireland in that year. Many British drivers travelled to Ireland for the fortnight of motoring. Their number included one Charles Stewart Rolls, who took part in the Speed Trials in the days when he had yet to be introduced to Henry Royce on the road to the Rolls-Royce partnership. It was a fortnight that included the Gordon Bennett race on 2 July, which was run over a course based around Athy in County Kildare. That race run, attention moved on the following day to Phoenix Park and the setting of new speed records.

Some 300 vehicles were entered for the 1903 trials and both motor cars and motorbikes were allowed to participate, though the quality and expertise of the participants must have been quite varied. Committed engineers and mechanics and wealthy owners participated cheek-by-jowl with have-a-go enthusiasts.

Entrants came in by Castleknock Gates and parked while they awaited their turn to speed off down the empty and inviting Chesterfield Avenue. That avenue is a straight road of good width along a distance of almost two miles. Designed as a tree-lined avenue, many of the trees planted in the time of Lord Chesterfield in the mid-eighteenth century had been blown down six months earlier, in January, in the Great Wind that swept away some 3,000 park trees in one storm. However, by the time of the race, the debris had been cleared from the road and speed trials could be conducted in relative safety.

Cars assembled between Castleknock Gate and Mountjoy Cross. Motorbikes assembled along Whitefields Road while they awaited their opportunity to turn onto Chesterfield Avenue. A safety barrier was placed across the road beyond the finish line to prevent encroachment by vehicles or over-enthusiastic spectators. Onlookers were kept behind wooden barriers outside a strip some fifteen metres wide on either side of the road, and all was set.

Drivers travelled down the park's main road over a course of one mile, measured from a standing start at Mountjoy Cross, and a further flying kilometre thereafter. That way, hurtling drivers had some 350 metres in which to slow down before meeting Gough on his immovable stone horse once they had completed their speed trial. Gough's Corner is the nearest crossroads to Parkgate Street on the way into Dublin city. Contestants, once they had completed the run, drove past the Police Depot on the Back Road and out of the park to re-enter at Castleknock Gate for the next heat, if they had qualified.

Phoenix Column, which stood in the middle of the road, was slimmed down by removing its outlying railings and lights and allowing the core monument to stand in the path of the racing cars. Contestants steered past it and carried on their way. The monument was moved to a side road some years later when full motor racing came to Phoenix Park, but for the speed trials it was simply a feature of the course.

While the speeds achieved may be no more than modern motorists might attain on a clear motorway, it would have taken some considerable determination to drive at such speeds in early cars and motorbikes, with no rollover bars or any of the safety features taken for granted nowadays in family saloons, never mind in modern racing cars.

According to racing historian Bob Montgomery, writing in his book *Racing in the Park*, competing cars were brought to the starting line two at a time side-by-side in fine dry weather, with the exception of cars entered in the racing car class. These cars, which were considerably faster than the other cars, were sent off one-by-one to give them the greatest amount of room during their runs, for safety considerations. Motorcycles started either three or four at a time in each heat.

Of the more than 300 entrants, most were motorcycles, and to accommodate everybody, three motorcycle classes were run. The fastest motorbike speed, 48.2 miles per hour, on the day was achieved by C.G. Garrard riding a Clement-Garrard.

However, as much of a success as the speed trials were, permission was refused in 1904 for another round of trials in Phoenix Park, even though some 30,000 spectators are thought to have attended the 1903 event. In fact, more than a quarter of a century was to pass before racing resumed in Phoenix Park, by which time a national armed rebellion had occurred, followed by a war of independence and the setting up of the Irish Free State (Saorstát Éireann), and the passing of the 1925 Phoenix Park Act.

With the country somewhat settled once more, an official announcement was made, in January 1929, that motor racing would take place that summer in the park under the auspices of the Royal Irish Automobile Club and would include an international entry.

To create an uninterrupted straight this time, the Phoenix Column was moved to a new location to the side of the road, where it remained for many decades before being moved back again to its present location on the roundabout. A stretch of Chesterfield Avenue from Mountjoy Cross still forms part of the motor-racing circuit today, but the cars turn off before they meet the Phoenix Column and its roundabout.

The 1929 races, held in July, were a success on all levels and the new Free State Government under W.T. Cosgrave supported the races. In fact, £3,000 was given by the Government as grant-in-aid for the expenses of the Royal Irish Automobile Club in connection with the International Motor Races.

The races were repeated in 1930 and 1931 while Cosgrave's government was in power. In 1930, closure of a public park for all but motor racing had become the subject of discussion in the Dáil when Seamus Aloysius Bourke, Parliamentary Secretary to the Minister for Finance, told the then opposition speakers that it was not practicable to arrange that citizens and others not interested in motor racing could have access to the Zoological and People's Flower Gardens during the race times, without having to pay a charge for entering the park. "The difficulty caused by the persons who have a right of free admission to the park through residence or occupation is considerable, but it would clearly be impracticable to admit everyone who said he was going to the Zoological Gardens or the People's Gardens," said Bourke, adding that the government was acting under the powers of the 1925 Act.

The general election of 1932 returned a Fianna Fáil government led by Eamon de Valera, who made it clear that it would not continue to support what it described as a rich man's game, and the RIAC decided it could not sustain such a large outlay as the international races had required. The Irish Motor Racing Club (IMRC) took over the running of the annual event on a reduced scale thereafter.

In 1939, the races went ahead as scheduled, on 9 September, despite the official outbreak of war between Britain and Germany on 3 September. Unsurprisingly, no entries were received from British drivers that year and a motorcycle race was run in conjunction with the motor car races to fill out the programme.

With the world engulfed in turmoil and the park pressed into service as a vast fuel dump, motor racing halted in Phoenix Park until 1949, by which time the Free State had given way to the Irish Republic, which came into effect on Easter Monday, 18 April 1949. Two days before the Republic was born, motor racing returned to the park on 16 April with a sprint event organised by IMRC. The war may have been over, and the young republic about to be whelped, but the drivers were still racing between high stacks of turf held in storage from wartime rationing. The highest speed achieved that year was 65.4 miles per hour by C.E. Robb in a Mercury.

With some exceptions, motor racing has continued each year in Phoenix Park since then and large parts of the park are closed down for several days to facilitate the races.

From 1950 onwards, the IMRC organised a short circuit for racing and there were sufficient entries to ensure the races went ahead. The 1950s brought mixed fortune to the races, as economic hardship in general led to a lowering of entries. By 1956, petrol rationing brought about by the Suez Canal crisis in the Middle East conspired against running race meetings and permission could not be obtained for full-scale racing in Phoenix Park. However, the IMRC did receive approval for a half-mile event. By 1959, economic life had recovered sufficiently to see a return of motor racing to Phoenix Park. Races were held on just one day, a Saturday, with practice being held on the previous Thursday and Friday mornings from 6.00 am to 8.00 am.

By 1967, the event was restored to a two-day meeting where it continued to thrive and draw both sufficient entries and spectators alike. The 1960s saw the appearance in the park of powerful motors like the Lola T70, the Ferrari 250LM, Ford's GT40, and the Formula 1 Lotus, and Cooper. They were followed in the 1970s by F1, F5000 and Formula Atlantic cars.

However, continuing development of the park and wear and tear on roads arising from increased commuter traffic from the developing hinterland saw extensive roadworks being undertaken and in 1987 such was the extent of the disruption that motor racing could not be undertaken, though lack of funds were also a factor.

A year earlier a five-year park development plan had addressed the issue of closing the park to accommodate motor racing. "Phoenix Park is in principle an unsuitable location for such an event, as it cannot be reconciled with basic park objectives or with peaceful enjoyment of the amenities of the Park by other visitors," said the

Danner and Nannini set off on a demo run in Phoenix Park, 1997

report. "If the opportunity should arise for the event to transfer to another location this would be welcomed. For so long as the event continues to be held in Phoenix Park, with the support of the general public, it will be held on a fixed circuit and with adequate regulations governing safety and protection of Park resources and amenities."

Racing returned in 1988 and continued, with the exception of 1992, in the 1990s. In 1992, a smaller-scale car and motorcycle drag meet was run between the Phoenix Column and Montjoy Cross, in a joint promotion with the Munster Motorcycle and Light Car Club. Following the failure of the 1992 meeting to go ahead, IMRC combined with the Leinster Motor Club to rejuvenate the annual event.

Rothmans, the tobacco company, sponsored the park races between 1995 and 1997 and those years saw Formula 1 stars Damon Hill and Jacques Villeneuve appear on the circuit. Damon Hill was popular with the crowds and drove demonstration laps in a Renault Spider in 1996, making more than one enthusiast's heart beat a flutter with the sight and sound of the machine tearing through the deer park of Ormond and Chesterfield. An F1 Williams was demonstrated by Jean Christopher Bouillon.

Their presence brought huge crowds, numbering by now in the hundreds of thousands, back to the park. Sellers of confectionery, ice cream and motoring knick-knacks of all sorts set out their stalls for consideration by the milling crowds while commentary on the racing drivers flying past was relayed on the public address system and the races became a social occasion in addition to the sporting event that it is. By then, the races had gathered large amounts of ancillary equipment and personnel and the flat lands of Whitefields north of Chesterfield Avenue had become the assembly and pit area.

Park speeds increased over the years and two Alfa Romeo 155 touring cars reached a top speed of 168 miles per hour by the early 1990s, nine decades after the Phoenix Park speed trials saw a world speed record of 85.9 miles per hour being set.

In July 2000 a six-lap demonstration of the Jordan 193 Formula One racing car was given by Sarah Kavanagh, Ireland's top female driver. A major motorbike demonstration featuring six ex-world champions — Phil Read, Ralph Bryans, Tommy Robb, Sammy Miller, Jim Redman and Luigi Taveri — took place on the Sunday afternoon when the vets gave a demonstration of their motorcycling skills to the enthusiastic attendance.

The 2001 meeting went ahead following the easing in June of national restrictions created by a national foot and mouth scare earlier in the year.

Also in 2001, the official opening of nearby Farmleigh House to the public forced the race organisers to run a week earlier than planned. That same year, a new set of stamps was issued to commemorate Irish motor racing events. The stamps included depictions of cars that had raced in Phoenix Park since 1930. The Mercedes SSK that featured on the £1 stamp was the winner of the 1930 Irish Grand Prix. The Mini Cooper S on the 45p stamp was driven by Paddy Hopkirk in the Monte Carlo Rally. Hopkirk was also a park racer in his time. A Jordan Grand Prix Formula 1 car was shown on the high-selling 30p stamp.

In 2002, Dúchas, the Heritage Service, which administered the park that year, postponed a major resurfacing of Chesterfield Avenue to the end of 2002, because of funding arrangements. The races were again cancelled due to lack of funds. Motorsport Ireland set aside €100,000 for work on resurfacing parts of the circuit, but said the monies allocated to resurfacing the roads in effect meant it had no additional funding available to support a race meeting in the Park that year.

The 2005 race meeting did not go ahead for want of sufficient sponsorship, but the IMRC are confident that racing will resume in 2006.

Variety in the RJB Mining Race in 1997: a Crossle leads a Chevron followed by The Ark Sprite out of Mountjoy Corner

While contestants must pay for the privilege of entering the park, spectators pay nothing at all to participate in the great festival of racing that is the Phoenix Park motor races.

PHOENIX PARK RACECOURSE

Dublin city was a smaller place geographically when the Phoenix Park Racecourse was in its heyday. However, with the spread of the city out and beyond its Ashtown home, the land the racecourse stood upon was bound to be more valuable as a site for housing development than for the galloping of horses every now and then. Opened as a racecourse in 1902, one hundred years later the racecourse had closed, the stables were no more and apartments were arising on the once green sward. But, while it stood, the Phoenix Park racecourse played its part in the sporting life of the city, though it lay outside Phoenix Park proper and did not come under the jurisdiction of the OPW.

A programme of quality racing put the emphasis on speed in the park racecourse. The annual Phoenix Plate for two-year-olds was held over five furlongs until 1913 and was the richest race in the country, surpassing even the Irish Derby at the time.

Two world wars tempered travel around the country in pursuit of horse-racing in the first half of the twentieth century and many large trainers and stables remained in the vicinity of Dublin city. The racecourse came into its own then as an attraction for racegoers and the racing industry alike.

Some trainers used a designated gallop across the Fifteen Acres in Phoenix Park, under licence, to train racehorses. Though the gallop, running from west to east on the southern side of the Fifteen Acres, is still there, it has fallen into disuse now that most of the stables have moved away to quieter areas of the country, and the racecourse is no more.

Such was the popularity of the races in their day that a section of Whitefields just inside the Ashtown Gates of Phoenix Park was allocated for race-day motor car parking. A park regulation still expressly forbids stopping or parking cars on the adjacent park roads on race-days.

The racecourse reached the height of its popularity in the 1950s, but by the early 1980s it had been sold to property developer Patrick Gallagher. Once a major mover in housing development in Dublin, Gallagher's firm faded as a property developer and the racecourse was sold on without development being pursued on the site.

Members of a racing syndicate became the new owners and they sought to extend the wider facility by introducing ancillary activities including discos, bars and other leisure facilities. There was even a garden centre and a weekend market on the site at various times. However, though the syndicate invested considerable funds to improve the course, it failed to take off.

Maintaining high prizes, the final Phoenix Park fixture in the autumn of 1990 saw the running of the world's richest race for two-year-olds, the Cartier Million, which the jewellers and Goffs

Bloodstock Sales joined forces to sponsor and promote. The racecourse had been refurbished at great expense two years earlier, but meetings did not attract the expected crowds. Even the running of the Cartier Million drew a crowd of just 5,000 spectators and a small field even though the purse was substantial. Racing was discontinued on the racecourse in October 1990.

New owners, Ogden Leisure, an American corporation, under the project title of Sonas abandoned the racecourse element but failed to achieve planning permissions for a €476 million leisure development, including a national conference centre, multi-purpose stadium and a large casino in its stead. The proposal for a casino in particular aroused widespread opposition. The company said it needed permission for a full gaming casino to ensure the financial viability of the entire project. Politicians were lobbied by the company to relax stringent gaming laws to facilitate the plan.

But, while the developers did achieve planning approval, following an appeal to An Bord Pleanála, the Rainbow Government, led by John Bruton TD, was not willing to change the gaming laws. Bertie Ahern TD, as opposition Fianna Fáil leader, told the Dáil in May 1997 that he was opposed to a casino on the site. With all sides against relaxing gaming laws, the project was abandoned.

The present developers Flynn & O'Flaherty then bought the property for a reported £37 million from the previous owners and successfully applied for planning permission on the 125-acre site for more than 2,300 dwelling units and supporting services, including a 200-bedroom hotel, a neighbourhood shopping centre with restaurants and bars and twenty-five acres of sporting and leisure facilities.

The hotel was designed to occupy the site of the ruined nineteenth-century Arnott's house, beside the Ashtown roundabout. Quality homes were planned for the site in recognition of the unique location of the old racecourse, beside the park, near the Tolka River valley and within walking robust walking distance of the city.

Sadly, while the racecourse and its buildings were unoccupied, vandals set fires in the buildings in 1998. The former home of the Arnott family was attacked, as was a grandstand near the Navan Road. There were eight fires set at the former racecourse in a nine-month period while it lay idle.

Worse was to come when a mix-up at local authority level saw demolition of a protected structure take place in 1999. Agreement had been reached with the racecourse owners on the extent of works which included demolition of the stands and the buildings necessary to render the area safe following the fires. But turnstiles and the racecourse gate lodge were also demolished. When the mistake became apparent, the developers offered to carry out the reconstruction on its own account.

The structures did not have preservation orders but the local area action plan, which regulates planning in a designated area, had recommended preservation of existing features if development were to take place. While council officials had advised the developers to carry out safety work to buildings with dangerous building notices placed on them, the council's conservation officer was not notified by his colleagues of the pending demolitions until after the event, according to council management.

However, with planning turmoil in the past and the site cleared, the old racecourse is now home to a new community of residents who count themselves lucky to live within a stone's throw of the biggest enclosed park in Europe and to have the park and its facilities as a personal pleasure garden, even if horses' hooves no longer race across the old racecourse.

As the tempo of modern life speeds up, it is well to know that Phoenix Park and its sports facilities are there for all to enjoy. Competitive or recreational, the park welcomes all movers and shakers.

9

DUBLIN ZOO

Dublin Zoo was established in 1831 when the Lord Lieutenant who ruled Ireland on behalf of the King of England granted the new Zoological Society use of a portion of Phoenix Park for the purpose of creating a menagerie.

The Zoological Gardens of the 1830s was nothing like it is today. On opening day there was just one wild boar to be seen — and that was it, but in its day it would have been a wild and exotic creature to see. Other species followed and today's visitor is spoilt for choice across more than sixty acres of the modern Zoo.

Originally the area for the Zoo was three and a half acres in extent with about four acres of water on its boundary. There were a lodge, some outhouses and a small cottage on the allocated land. In 1830, an approach was made to the architect to London Zoo, Decimus Burton, to prepare plans for Phoenix Park. Burton did so for a fee of £75. His plan called for enclosing part of the neighbouring lake and the expansion into some of the adjacent land. However, the plan was beyond the financial capacity of the young Zoological Society to implement, and was eventually used merely as a guide for later development.

During the following years, the lay-out of the Gardens was supervised by many others, including Sir Frederick Moore, Director of the Botanical Gardens. One person whose presence had a major impact on the form of the Gardens was Robert Lloyd Praegar, one-time President of the Society. The present appearance of the Zoo owes much to his foundation work, since built on with skill and diligence by the gardening staff of Dublin Zoo.

In 1830, King William IV presented to the Zoological Society of London all the animals in the Royal Menagerie in Windsor Great Park, which was being disbanded at that time. Some that were surplus to the London zoo's requirements were given to Dublin. Amongst these were two wapiti deer, a sambun deer, one nylghai, two emus, two ostriches and some animals of lesser importance in zoological pecking order. At the end of 1831 the Zoological Society of London presented to Dublin Zoo a lioness, a cub, a striped hyena, a male leopard, and a wolf, some of which may have originated in the King's collections.

The operations of the Society were on a modest scale for the first few years after the gardens formally opened on 1 September 1831. Early stock included forty-six mammals, of which fifteen were monkeys, and seventy-two birds.

Up to 1840, charges for admission were either three old pence or six old pence, but in 1841 an admission price of a penny was introduced as a marketing measure and more than 81,000 people each spent a penny in that year for entrance to the Zoo. The move to penny admission and its attraction to the populace enabled the Society to continue in operation.

In 1844, the Zoo received its first giraffe and in 1855 it bought its first pair of lions. These bred for the first time in 1857. Dublin Zoo has had some success with the breeding of lions. In fact, from 1857 to 1965, some 593 cubs were born in Dublin Zoo, more than in any other zoo in the world.

As early as 1835 a public subscription list was opened for the purpose of providing an elephant to the Zoo, but the funds offered were not sufficient to meet the cost. Dublin then made application to the Zoological Society of London for a female elephant on unique terms. Dublin would bring her over at the expense of the Dublin Zoological Society and the London Society could take her, or her

The African lion: one of the great success stories of Dublin Zoo

skeleton, when they pleased. The live elephant arrived and was duly housed in a special enclosure erected for the purpose. When the elephant died, in 1842, her skeleton was prepared and exhibited to the public.

Reptiles got their own house in 1876 and the first tearooms for humans were built in 1898.

The original purpose of the Zoo was to show as many different kinds of animals as possible to people who had never seen their likes before. Sadly, that meant caging animals so that humans could for the most part gaze and poke fun at the fierce, savage wild animals behind stout iron bars. The cages were small and gloomy, usually housing only one animal each and were in general use for many years.

A move was made away from such depressing enclosures when, starting in 1909, some cages with heavy iron bars were rebuilt using wire mesh instead of bars. The change meant lions, tigers and panthers had a relatively unimpeded view of the free world. In 1905, different species were placed in the same enclosures for variety. Present practice is to place family or social groups together. Much use is made in modern zoos of invisible barriers like moats, glass and wire mesh to give the impression that the animals are roaming free in open parkland, at peace with one another.

There is a point of view, often forcefully expressed, that animals should not be restrained in a zoo at all but should be allowed live their span of life in their natural habitat. However, during the twentieth century it became obvious that many habitats and animals were disappearing in their traditional environments. Many zoos became centres for conservation, education and study. Animals in captivity have been shown to live longer than their counterparts in the wild.

Dublin Zoo is part of a worldwide network of zoos working together to breed endangered species. Studbooks are used to manage this captive breeding. Dublin Zoo holds the European studbooks for species including the Moluccan cockatoo and the golden lion tamarin. The Zoo also sponsors field research to study a group of tamarins that have been released back into protected habitats.

In common with the wider Phoenix Park many matters beyond the control of the Zoo have conspired to intrude on the Zoo and its existence. The First World War saw attendances fall below a sustainable level as fewer people traveled to Ireland from Britain and Zoo visits fell. Street fighting during the 1916 Rebellion meant the park was isolated from food supplies and some weaker and older animals were killed to feed the others.

During the Second World War a German bomb exploded 150 metres from the Zoo boundary, causing damage to the Zoo buildings, but no casualties were sustained. Also during the war, trees were cut down to keep animal houses warm as a result of cold weather and a shortage of solid fuel. In the late twentieth century financial deficits meant the State had to make a grant to the Zoo to defray its debts.

Fallout from international and national affairs has not been all one-way, however. A claim to international fame for Dublin Zoo was the lion Cairbre born in the Zoo on 20 March 1927. He was the lion who roared on the opening of the Metro-Goldwyn-Mayer films. Back home in the park a son of Cairbre named Stephen became sire to seventy-seven cubs. Born in an outdoor enclosure on 26 December 1941, he was originally identified as a lioness and called Stephanie. When the mistake was discovered he was renamed Stephen, after St Stephen, on whose feast day he was born, and showed no lasting effect of being misgendered for some time, happily thereafter fathering his share of progeny.

While lions need a deal of space for their family recreation, birds can be housed relatively easily, and exotic birds make for good visual content, not to mention the effects of their unusual calls on the ear. Birds have been a popular attraction since the Zoo first

Familiar faces: Chilean flamingos at the Zoo

opened. Flightless birds like the ostrich, the rhea, the cassowary, and the kiwi have been particularly well received by Zoo visitors.

In the 1877 annual report it was recorded that Miss Nesbitt of Leixlip House, Leixlip, "completed, at a cost of upwards of £350, and handed over to the charge of the Zoo a handsome aviary promised in the previous report". Miss Nesbitt is recorded as a Life Member in the membership list and her name appears up to 1885.

As a barometer of the Zoo and its travails, the Nesbitt House featured quite a lot in reports. In 1903, damage to the roof from the Great Storm necessitated major repair. In 1919, the roof again needed reconstruction at cost of £500, though the entire original building had only cost £350 to build. In 1944, the building was overhauled and the outside flights altered. Further alterations were carried out in 1952, 1959 and 1966. And in 1986, for the visit of the pandas the shop was repainted in black and white and renamed the Panda Shop.

Outside, bird activity has continued apace with the Zoo's lakes, which provide a refuge for wildfowl, being the main focus. In modern times, and in winter, more than 500 wildfowl have been seen at close quarters from the public paths that overlook the lakes.

The Big Lake and African Plains Lake have a depth of some nine metres with narrow shallow margins. The Small Lake is shallow, with a maximum depth of only 1.8 metres. The African Plains Lake contains native marginal and aquatic plants, and much of the surrounding land includes a variety of mainly native semi-natural canopy trees, shrub layer, herb layer and some grassland, according to a paper prepared by Peter Phillips of the Zoo's bird department, who drew on his own and Sean Geraty's records to produce a list of seventy-five species of wild birds recorded in the Zoo during the past two decades.

Since the Zoo first opened for business, there have been a number of turnstile entrances in use. All three are still standing, although the latest building work dwarfs the other two, which are not used now but which may still be seen on the Zoo Road. The

The original thatched entrance lodge to the Zoo

oldest entrance is a cottage with a thatched roof designed and built with a strict budget of less than £30. The entrance was in the style of a mock-Tudor cottage. Beside it stands a mid-twentieth century utilitarian-design entrance through which the attractions of the Zoo may be glimpsed.

However, in 1999 the Irish architects Scott Tallon Walker conceived the award-winning entrance that greets visitors today. The same firm designed and supervised the building of the Papal Cross and altar on the Fifteen Acres for the 1979 papal visit. The modern Zoo entrance building was built further along the road from the two previous entrances. It is certainly different to earlier entrances with a roof designed to float over the solid lower walls, aided by the positioning of the walls and glazing used in its design.

The entrance building is a single-storey pavilion, which forms a walled edge to the public domain of the park. It contains a retail outlet, an entrance area with ticket kiosks, and a cash office with staff facilities. The separate built elements are unified by a single, over-sailing steel flat roof structure with an American white oak timber soffit, supported on ten slender circular-finned steel columns. The design won an award in 2000 when it was selected for exhibition by the Royal Institute of the Architects of Ireland.

Dublin Zoo has prospered in recent years and such is the press for tickets on good days that visitors have ample time to study the soaring roof design. Once inside, some other architectural sights may be observed. Zoological Society House itself is much overlooked by visitors to the Zoo; it is a solid large house with round-headed windows on its first floor.

Haughton House was built in 1898 as the Haughton Memorial Restaurant and designed by L.M. McDonnell. The original building is surrounded by later extensions, but architectural detail around the roof and eaves can still be observed. The original house was designed in a half-timbered neo-Tudor style.

McDonnell also designed the animal house known as Roberts House in a style that would have been familiar to late-nineteenth-century strollers. A decorative brick exterior masks a toplit interior space with Victorian ironwork for embellishment. Off the main block is a smaller block with external cages, where animals were placed for observation by visitors standing outside in the fresh air.

In 2005, Dublin Zoo opened the new 325-seater Meerkat Restaurant to ensure the Zoo experience is carried into the restaurant. A meerkat exhibit has been placed inside the restaurant. Meerkats are active during the day and the exhibit offers opportunity to learn about meerkats while dining.

By now, Dublin Zoo is one of the oldest zoos in the world. It is acknowledged to be one of the most beautiful of national zoos because of its location in extensive parkland and its landscaped aspect around a central lake. It also enjoys the great advantage of being convenient to a major populated city. It is relatively easy for people from everywhere, native and tourist alike, to have access to the Zoo.

As the national zoo it has a role to play not envisaged when the Zoo was founded in 1830 as a menagerie. Dublin Zoo has developed an education programme targeted at schools, and particularly primary school children, but which also covers secondary schools and third-level institutions. The education programme is aimed at stimulating interest in animals and in global conservation issues, and at disseminating information that will make the visitor more conscious of the threat that all animals are under.

Dublin Zoo is also a major tourist attraction and a recreation and general amenity attraction in its own right. That attraction creates its own problems for park management and pedestrians attempting to cross the busy road when parked cars of Zoo visitors combine with day-long commuter parking on Chesterfield Avenue to form long solid lines of parked cars on either side of the main road.

In 1994, the then Minister for Finance, Bertie Ahearn TD approved a massive £15 million (€19 million) ten-year plan for the Zoo. In the preceding years the Zoo had been the subject of much comment by animal welfare organisations. The 1990 Doyle Report, a government-funded report into the Zoo's operations, had also been critical of operations at the Zoo. It pointed out that Dublin Zoo's funding was totally inadequate and the consequent lack of facilities had caused distress particularly to the larger animals in the Zoo over recent years.

These points were addressed at the launch of the plan and the Zoo's director promised that under the development plan there would be a first class zoo in the park within five years. The development plan was drawn up by the Zoological Society of Ireland and the Office of Public Works. Junior Minister for Finance Noel Dempsey TD told the Dáil on 12 October 1993 that he had indicated four objectives for a development plan for the Zoo: to continue the captive breeding of endangered species and the presentation of species to foster an appreciation of nature and global conservation; to achieve animal care which meets the highest international standards within appropriate space requirements; to contribute to the tourism and recreational potential of Dublin by providing quality visitor facilities and programmes; and to operate to commercial standards so that State subsidies could be minimised.

One of the primary animal welfare recommendations of the Doyle Report was the addition of extra land. Consequently some thirty-two acres — "The African Plains" — were added to the Zoo to provide much-needed space for African species. The extra land was taken from the grounds of Áras an Uachtaráin. The first part of the extension of the Zoo onto the new land opened on 1 June 2000. The new area incorporates the African Plains where animals of African origin have room to roam somewhat more freely, though human visitors are protected from the animals by fencing. Since the extension of the African Plains, the dwell time at Dublin Zoo has increased to an average of three and a half hours.

Expansion into what was part of Áras an Uachtaráin's 200-acre grounds resulted in the narrowing of the Spa Road as a through road for motor cars, though a cycle lane and pedestrian route remain. The move was not without some controversy at the time, as are any proposals to close park roads to motor traffic, all of which attract dissent from motorists. Spa Road formed a boundary and break between the Zoo grounds and that of Áras an Uachtaráin, before the Zoo expanded. It is named for the well of spa water from which the park may also have taken its name.

Some years before the Zoo spread into Áras an Uachtaráin, the former Lord Mayor of Dublin Tomás MacGiolla TD, suggested, in 1991, that it would be "marvellous" to have giraffes and other animals from Dublin Zoo on Ashtown Castle grounds. The fifty-five-acre Ashtown Demesne wherein stands Ashtown Castle and the Visitor Centre is surrounded by a sunken fence designed by Decimus Burton in the nineteenth century, which would prevent the animals from wandering away through the park. However, thus far, his suggestion has not been proceeded with, though park deer graze in the lush grounds of the castle and Visitor Centre, as they do in Áras an Uachtaráin.

The first of the £15 million (€19 million) investment in the Zoo was spent improving animal enclosures. The Zoo redevelopment programme for 2002-2006 involved a number of separate projects: improved public/visitor facilities; the upgrade of support facilities; the upgrade of existing infrastructure; an ibis cliff exhibit; a new elephant house and outdoor exhibit. The provision of a new rock-effect cliff face exhibit for the critically endangered bald-headed ibis was nearing completion in 2005. The construction provides nesting areas and recreates the natural habitat for these birds. Public viewing areas were designed to minimise disturbance to the birds. A deck with panoramic views over the lake was included in the design.

In 2005, two ageing female Asian elephants named Judy and Kirsty, who came in 1993 to Dublin from Chester in England, were moved to Neunkirchen Zoo in Germany, leaving Dublin Zoo without an elephant to its name. A new elephant facility was designed to be fifty per cent larger than the older house and to incorporate a

Mother and baby Californian sea lions

riverbed and a large pool for the elephants. Landscaping would recreate the atmosphere of an Asian rainforest. Rotterdam Zoo offered to send a breeding group to Dublin when the new facility was ready. It was planned that two adults would be pregnant when they travelled. A bull elephant would be brought in to continue the breeding programme, once the females were settled in Dublin, according to the plan.

In addition to animal attractions, there is the magnificent setting of the Zoo's grounds, with sweeping views across the park and away to the Dublin mountains in the distance. Planting around the boundary of some enclosures acts as an additional deterrent to keep people away from the more dangerous animals. The planting of specimen trees in the animal enclosures can provide shelter for the animals. In any case, a well-placed tree or shrub can provide that element of surprise around every corner of the Zoological Gardens.

To keep the Gardens looking as well as they do, teams of gardeners are kept busy all year round. In spring, weed-spraying is conducted against the coming growing season. The lake is dredged to prevent it filling up with rotted leaves fallen from deciduous trees in autumn. New plants are propagated for planting the following year. In summer, grass is cut at least once a week. Sweeping up of litter after humans is a full-time job in itself, especially in summer. In autumn and winter hedges are pruned, and paths treated to clear moss.

Dublin Zoo can be visited without even leaving home. A website, www.dublinzoo.ie, contains details of all of the attractions at the Zoo including the African Plains extension. Full details of the Zoo's attractions, prices and opening times are listed on the website.

Changes and improvements and implementation of modern marketing have worked to the Zoo's betterment, as the numbers of returning visitors will attest, and Dublin Zoo is set fair for a bright and rewarding future, having travelled a long way from a single boar in the nineteenth century.

10

FLORA AND FAUNA

hoenix Park is a prime example of a seventeenth-century deer park. It was established within its present boundaries between 1662 and 1680. Through the centuries the park has transformed from being an outlying country estate to being an integral part of the capital city. To maintain the integrity of the park as it is today, many attempts by conflicting outside interests have been resisted over the years. It currently faces pressure from commuter interests and local public representatives to allow more use of the park by motorised traffic on its way into the city.

However, current management objectives are to conserve a historic landscape character; to encourage appropriate recreational use and public appreciation; and to conserve natural values within the park.

The park landscape is dominated by grassland separated by clumps of trees, which may appear to be haphazardly grown, but which were planted to complement other aspects of the park. Some twenty-eight per cent of the area is under trees. However, as discussed elsewhere, Phoenix Park contains a number of important residences and institutions, together with important monuments and historic buildings. Between them, at 403 acres, these enclosures occupy some twenty-three per cent of the park's overall area. That's almost a quarter of the park where there is no public access.

Little wonder then that park management resists applications and proposals to allocate exclusive specific space for minority use. The management plan for Phoenix Park calls for the park to be developed for both passive and recreational uses. Nonetheless, a number of enclosures within the park are reserved for other than public use. Most are restricted for reasons of security and others simply because they are people's homes. Some, like St Mary's Hospital, are for patient care and allow restricted access to visitors, and others, like the Ordnance Survey, are working areas which allow some public access. Dublin Zoo is perhaps the best known of the enclosures where access is allowed, though it is a controlled access with an entrance fee levied at the entry.

In Thomas Sherrard's Map of 1772, there is an enclosed area named as Fifteen Acres, which lay towards the western end of the meadowland. Although this area is no longer enclosed, the name Fifteen Acres is now used to refer to a much larger area of about 200 acres.

ADMINISTRATION AND MAINTENANCE AREAS

The nine-acre park superintendent's office and stores at Whitefields between Castleknock and Ashtown Gates is home to the Park Superintendent, in addition to being a large storage area for plant and material and the park's administrative hub. It is not open to the public, nor are the park's greenhouses, for instance, which are located in a secluded corner of the park known as the Klondike at the other end of the park. This area is situated just inside the main gates at Parkgate Street and is named for the area of Canada where a gold rush took place in 1897. Ever since they were built in the late nineteenth century, the glasshouses have been used for the growing of plants for the People's Flower Gardens across the road on the other side of Chesterfield Avenue. Thousands of plants are produced each year on the seven-acre site to decorate

Freshly planted flowers in the People's Flower Gardens

Leinster House, Dublin Castle and the Royal Hospital in nearby Kilmainham, and for general park use.

A stone tablet indicates that evergreen oaks growing within the enclosure were donated in 1904 by Sir Arthur Edward Guinness, who presented some 800 specimens which were grown from seed collected in 1887. The Guinness name is associated with both ends of the park, in fact. The estate at Farmleigh opening onto the south-western corner was a Guinness family home and the famous Dublin brewery across the river is a short distance from the main gates at Parkgate Street at the eastern end of the park.

Other enclosures arise when various plantations of trees are from time to time fenced off in Phoenix Park to allow young trees to grow, and to prevent deer from chewing on the young shoots. One area where young trees are currently protected is a 1990s plantation close to the Furry Glen where a deer fence was erected to keep the animals out while new trees grew to strength. The trees will ultimately be used to re-plant woodland in the neighbouring Oldtown Wood where specimens planted in the middle of the nineteenth century have reached maturity and are decaying. Oldtown Wood lies between Deerfield House, home to the US Ambassador, and the Ordnance Survey, forming a northern boundary to the 200 open acres of the Fifteen Acres. Sponsorship was introduced to encourage the public to contribute to the upkeep and development of the park through re-planting. The cost of re-planting a square metre of woodland in Phoenix Park was costed at £20 (€25) in the mid-1990s. Sponsors' names are entered on the park records in Ashtown Castle Visitor Centre as part of the promotion. The plan was to develop some 100,000 square metres with up to 10,000 broadleaf trees, including replacement oaks, beech, ash and sycamore. Horse chestnuts are to be planted as well, according to the master plan.

PONDS, WOODLANDS AND OPEN AREAS

Trees have also been planted over the years as screens around a number of ponds in Phoenix Park. There are trees around the pond at Citadel (the Dog Pond) located between Phoenix and Civil Service Cricket grounds south of Chesterfield Avenue, near the Zoo. There is the nearby People's Flower Gardens pond; the Quarry lake with an island, situated beside Mountjoy crossroads near Castleknock gate; and the more famous Furry Glen pond, which is fed from Baker's Well, located near Knockmaroon Gate in the south-west corner.

Woods planted and now open to access include Bishop's Wood, which is part of the People's Flower Gardens; a Black Wood of thorn trees south of the main road near to the Garda Athletic grounds; Pump Wood near the thorn wood between the Khyber and Acres Road not far from the Papal Cross; Ash Wood north of Castleknock Gate; and Butchers' Wood south of the same gate.

Half Mile Hollow, between the southern perimeter of the Fifteen Acres and the Chapelizod Road wall, was in 1925 suggested as part of a site for a large flower bed during the debate on the Phoenix Park Bill of that year. Donegal-born TD Joseph O'Doherty suggested that the area between Parkgate Street and Chapelizod, along the Magazine Road, being one of the most beautiful portions of the Park, would make a fine site for flower-growing allotments. "There is a considerable stretch of land between the Magazine Road and the wall which, on account of the slope there, would be ideal for allotments for flowers," he said. "One of the prettiest sights would be to see acre after acre of flowers grown there by the townspeople." Sadly, this proposal was never implemented.

CONSERVATION

Progress has been made in recent years towards restoration of tranquillity through phased extinguishment of minor roads, reduction of opening hours of side gates and even closure of some gates to vehicular traffic. Development of the wildlife area in the southwest of the park, focusing on the Furry or Furze Glen, is seen as part of passive recreational activities development.

The majority of soils in Phoenix Park afford poor natural drainage but are most suitable for growing a wide range of tree species. Soils in Phoenix Park are for the most part of a stiff, tenacious calcareous substance and of varying thickness. Small areas of gravel and alluvium appear near Chapelizod Gate and Knockmaroon Gate.

The preserved wildlife zone includes a defined nature trail, in addition to foot-worn paths through the leafy trees. Priority is given to wildlife conservation and habitat protection in this area. The management strategy here is to minimise the amount of landscape maintenance and encourage natural decay of fallen trees and growth of waterside plant communities. Trees lie where they fall, within safety considerations, and birds carry seeds and seedlings

Trees, flora and wildlife thrive around the park's lakes and ponds

to new locations. Natural regeneration of woodland is encouraged with an undergrowth of herb and shrub layers to provide a rich food and shelter source for bird and animal life.

Management strives to maintain and improve conservation strategies including deer management, woodland conservation, wildflower and grassland management, management of wetlands and even species management.

In this context, the grey squirrel, while it might be a cuddly-looking animal beloved of children and others alike, is causing problems for the park and its trees. A solution is being sought to lessen the effects of its stripping of the bark of mature trees in Phoenix Park.

Squirrels may be seen everywhere, and they tend to frolic on the grass and in the trees at Phoenix Park Visitor Centre. The centre includes a permanent exhibition on the flora and fauna of Phoenix Park for those who may not wish to tramp about in inclement

The grey squirrel: cuddly pet or troublsesome vermin?

weather. Of particular interest is a display in the Visitor Centre of modern wooden sculptures fashioned from the wood of various fallen trees of Phoenix Park.

TREES IN THE PARK

The park may appear as a wide-open expanse but some thirty per cent of the land surface is covered with trees, mainly broadleaf parkland species like oak, ash, lime, beech, sycamore and horse chestnut. The main avenue through the park is planted with lime, beech and horse chestnut. An avenue of limes and another of sycamore is growing along the Wellington Road and a short avenue of limes was planted to effect in front of Garda Headquarters on the Back Road. A small quantity of evergreen conifers was planted in the 1950s in the Furry Glen area and there are some older plantations scattered throughout the park. A more ornamental selection of trees grows within the various enclosures — Ashtown Castle, Áras an Uachtaráin, Ordnance Survey and the residence of the US Ambassador at Deerfield. Hawthorn plantations growing throughout the park give a dramatic visual and sensory effect in springtime when they release a heady perfume into the clear air in addition to providing food and shelter for wildlife.

Different varieties of yews are found in the vicinity of Ashtown Castle. Also present are specimens of blue atlas cedar native to Algeria and Morocco, and western red cedar native to North America from Alaska to California. The timber of the western red cedar is light and strong and was used by some Indian tribes for making canoes and totem poles.

The largest tree in Phoenix Park is a giant redwood, a native of the Sierra Nevada in California, measuring over thirty-one metres and planted near Ashtown Castle.

Sadly, Phoenix Park is not impervious to disease and some two thousand mature elm trees were felled in the 1980s as a result of Dutch elm disease, despite the best efforts of park management at the time to save the trees. Visually, the felling of so many trees had an adverse effect on some areas of the park. However, the consequences could have been much worse were it not that many groups of trees contained a mixture of species.

The only comparable loss of trees to a single cause was in 1903 when a storm lashed the entire country on the night of the big wind. Phoenix Park is a relatively elevated area and prone to storm damage. Some 2,948 trees were blown down that night and 1,242 forest trees and 1,706 thorns perished.

As can be seen, the majority of trees in Phoenix Park grow in woodland situations like the Oldtown Wood area, the Ordnance Survey and Sankey's Wood near the Garda Athletic Pavilion. Other woodlands include the Furry Glen, Ashwood and Butcher's Wood adjacent to the Castleknock entrance, Ashtown Castle demesne, Áras an Uachtaráin and Bishop's Wood in the People's Flower

Trees and their conservation are an important function of the park

Gardens. Oak woods are situated at the entrances to the Ordnance Survey and to Ashtown Castle.

Groups and clumps of trees are planted throughout the park and are noticeable along the Khyber and Upper Glen Roads. Groups of evergreen oaks were planted in the early 1900s along the Back Road and inside the Parkgate Street entrance, in the People's Flower Gardens and near the Wellington Monument, primarily to replace the trees blown down and uprooted in the 1903 storm.

A feature of tree planting in earlier times were "roundels" or round groups of both mixed and single species. They were planted particularly in the environs of the Oldtown Wood area and form an attraction of their own. They are unusual in having few species within the roundel and where a single species is planted most trees tend to be the same age and height unlike the tangled competing growth pattern of the wilderness area.

Children, such as these girl guides in the 1980s, are encouraged to think environmentally through the park's tree-planting programme

A modern programme of tree planting and tree care was initiated in Phoenix Park in 1985. Some 10,000 standard broadleaf trees conforming to the nineteenth-century landscape design of Decimus Burton have since been planted. The range of species corresponds to those used by Burton, much in evidence in the mature plantings visible in the park today.

When Heads of State visit Ireland, it is quite common that there be ceremonial plantings of trees at Áras an Uachtaráin, home of the President — continuing a tradition from the days of Queen Victoria, who planted an Irish oak in 1853. When US President John F. Kennedy visited Ireland in June 1963, he planted a giant redwood, as did President Eamon de Valera. Pope John Paul II planted an Irish oak on his visit in 1979. US President Ronald Reagan planted a magnolia in 1984, and King Juan Carlos of Spain planted a sweet chestnut in 1986. Japan's Emperor Akihito planted a Japanese Katsura in 1985 and on his return twenty years later on an official visit with his Empress Michiko was shown the grown tree and its progress in the intervening years. In 1991, President Mary Robinson planted a beech in the grounds of the residence.

OTHER FLORA

Wild plants have been observed and enjoyed in Phoenix Park for nearly 300 years, according to the Office of Public Works. The first records of the flora of the park were published during its early period as a royal deer park even before it was opened to the public in 1745. Several plants can still be found on or near the sites where they were first noted by Caleb Threlkeld in 1726, including gipsywort (near lake shores and in ditches); lords-and-ladies (in shady places); swine cress (on disturbed ground); hairy bitter cress (on walls); burnet saxifrage (in grassland); and holly (in the woods).

Considering that it is now an urban park, Phoenix Park supports a surprisingly rich flora. In fact, during a recent survey more than 300 different flowering grasses and ferns were recorded. That represents about a third of all the species found in Ireland, and some forty-four per cent of those to be found in the Dublin area. The large number is attributable to the variety of habitats, which are suitable for different kinds of plants.

The principal habitats are obviously open grassland, small lakes and wetlands, and deciduous woodland, but the park's eleven-kilometre-long boundary wall is also a habitat for flora, not surprisingly. The stone wall that runs around the entire perimeter of the park is three metres high. Apart from it being a practical barrier, the wall is a designated national monument in its own right. It also supports its own particular flora, which includes ivy-leaved toadflax and a number of ferns including wall-rue, maidenhair spleenwort, hart's-tongue fern, rustyback fern, Polypody fern and Black spleenwort, according to the OPW.

There are six small lakes and a number of marshy areas where interesting plants are generally to be found in the park including the white water lily, yellow water lily, starwort, duckweed, water fern, sweet grasses, water mint, angelica, marsh roundwort and great willowherb. They can be looked for in the Dog Pond, the Quarry Pond, the People's Flower Gardens, the ponds in Dublin Zoo and in the Glen Pond.

Small woods of deciduous woodland in all areas of the park are home to shade-loving plants which grow most profusely at the edge of woods. These include ground ivy, wood sanicle, broom rape, bluebell, enchanter's nightshade, false brome, wild garlic and violets.

While open grassland comprises the greater part of the park, there are no less than forty-two species of grass to be found together with broad-leaved flowering plants in Phoenix Park. Their evocative names alone justify a ramble across the grasslands to identify and wonder at the different species which include sweet

Various species of mushroom and other fungi can be found in the woods and grasslands such as at Whitefields

vernal grass, quaking grass, cocksfoot, rye-grass, crested dog's-tail and Timothy.

Flowering plants to be found in the grasslands include self-heal, silverweed, buttercup, black medick, creeping cinquefoil and pyramidal orchid. Three acres of Whitefields enclosure have even been set aside to encourage the growth of wild flora.

Not all pretty things are good for you, however. The acorn, much associated with the wise squirrel stashing away his nuts for winter sustenance, actually contains tannin which is toxic and avoided by most species. The arum lily, or lords-and-ladies, for its part is one of ten particular plants recorded by Caleb Threlkeld in Phoenix Park in 1726. An early spring plant, it is well established throughout the park in shady hedges and woods. Its bright scarlet berries, which are poisonous, appear in August and September.

Mind you, Threlkeld wrote that the arum lily is a native of Ireland, growing copiously in the counties of Dublin and Wicklow, and in the Phoenix Park belonging to his Majesty. "The roots, bruised and distilled with cows milk, makes a noble remedy for cleaning the skin from wrinkles, scruff, freckles, spots or blemishes whatsoever," said Threlkeld, though he neglected to say what the King thought of it as a cure for freckles and wrinkles.

BIRDS AND BIRDWATCHING

The phoenix is a fabled bird of Egyptian mythology, said to regenerate its life and to rise from the ashes of fire every 500 years. It is usually depicted as a large bird of prey with wings splayed and beak agape, surrounded by flames. The stone bird atop the Phoenix Monument on Chesterfield Avenue is as reasonable a rendition of a non-existent bird as any other.

However, students of bird behaviour are aware that many birds adopt this posture when in contact with a source of heat, including the smouldering embers of a fire. The rooks of Phoenix Park perch on top of the lighted gas lamps which line Chesterfield Avenue, and in cold weather may be seen performing the Phoenix Hop atop the lamps, as the lampshades beneath them heat up from the gas below while the stone phoenix gazes impassively down upon their antics.

For stone or human alike, Phoenix Park is an ideal location for bird-watching, with a wide range of habitats available — including its mature deciduous and evergreen trees, shrubs, seeding grasses and wild plants, rolling meadows, lawns and open water.

The 1938 annual report of the Commissioners of Public Works in Ireland stated: "Phoenix Park which heretofore was virtually a bird sanctuary is now officially recognised as such. Shooting of birds or taking of nests is punishable by a fine."

Under the current Phoenix Park Management Plan, the area near the western end is designated as a natural zone and includes the Furry Glen, an area much favoured by birdwatchers, with resident avian species including sparrowhawks, long-eared owls, little grebes and jays.

In an example of nature co-operating in propagation, jays carry acorns away in autumn from their parent oak trees and bury them by ramming them into the ground, for later consumption. A single jay will drive a group of magpies away in its search for acorns, such is its determination. If a bird forgets the location, dies, gets a better offer, or does not return for whatever reason, an abandoned acorn will be ready for spring growth of its own accord and an oak sapling will grow, often some distance from the parent tree.

According to Niall Hatch, BirdWatch Ireland Development Officer, the park supports a wide range of relatively common woodland and parkland bird species and is a particularly important Dublin site for breeding sparrowhawks. It also holds some breeding and wintering long-eared owls.

"One of the main reasons that birders would visit the park is to see the population of jays that live there," he said. "This shy and scarce member of the crow family is very seldom seen in the Dublin

A thrush, one of the regular inhabitants of the park

area, but is frequently encountered in the oak trees near to the Ordnance Survey Office."

Field trips by experienced members of the Irish Wildbird Conservancy have recorded more than ninety different species of birds in Phoenix Park, demonstrating the tremendous enjoyment available to all, at little cost in terms of money or time. For more information, visit www.birdwatchireland.ie.

Best places for birdwatching in wetland habitat are the Furry Glen pond, the People's Flower Gardens pond and the Quarry Lake. Wetland species to be seen may include little grebe, moorhen, heron, coot, mute swan, pied wagtail, mallard, grey wagtail and tufted duck. Less common are the gulls, including the black-headed, great black-backed, herring and common gulls, though when the Phoenix Park Extension across the river at Chapelizod was the city landfill dump in the 1960s, there were gulls aplenty to be seen. The land is settled there now and the gulls have departed.

Swans guarding their cygnets on the People's Garden Pond

Good areas to see woodland birds include the Furry Glen, Oldtown Wood, the Ordnance Survey Office Wood and the trees inside the boundary wall. Woodland birds that may be seen in Phoenix Park include the wren, bullfinch, goldcrest, spotted flycatcher, blue tit, blackbird, coal tit, song thrush, great tit, collared dove, long-tailed tit, stock dove, treecreeper, woodpigeon, chiffchaff, jay, willow warbler, magpie, blackcap, kestrel, dunnock, long-eared owl, robin, sparrowhawk, greenfinch and pheasant. The largest bird in the park is the mute swan and the smallest is the goldcrest.

Parkland birds may be sought on the Fifteen Acres, the sports fields, the Polo Grounds and the open area of Whitefields. Birds of open parkland include swift, swallow, house martin, meadow pipit, skylark, fieldfore, redwing, mistle thrush, jackdaw, rook, hooded crow, starling, house sparrow, chaffinch, goldfinch, linnet, redpoll and reed bunting. Less common are the merlin, oystercatcher and golden plover.

The Zoo grounds provide an excellent opportunity for enthusiasts with an interest in natural history to observe waterfowl at close quarters. In the early months of a year, more than 500 wildfowl can be seen at close quarters in Dublin Zoo from the public paths that overlook the ponds. However, the Zoo's collection of wildfowl is fed daily from three feeding stations, so it's moot as to whether they are wildfowl in the sense of a species fending for itself, without assistance from man. Nonetheless, the Zoo has recorded the presence of some seventy-five species of wild birds during the past fifteen years.

OTHER WILDLIFE

While the zoo is an attended reserve for animals and other species, the wider Phoenix Park is a sanctuary for many animals, including the fox whose park numbers rise and fall depending on the food available. When the myxomatosis disease ravaged the rabbit population, scarcity of food saw the number of foxes naturally decrease in Phoenix Park.

Areas that are not generally open to the public are uniquely important for conservation of wildlife. Badgers make their home in these safe areas where they do not have to tolerate interference from humans. The badger's home or sett usually consists of a series of holes and tunnels, in ditches or embankments, or under the roots of trees, and a badger entering in one place may emerge some distance away.

Like badgers' setts, fox dens are usually found beneath the roots of trees or in ditches. A fox may even take over an abandoned badger sett as its own; sometimes, they co-habit in an extended sett. Bones, feathers, fur and droppings are found outside a den when a fox is in residence, and can smell strongly. Within the park, the fox is most commonly found in restricted areas like Áras an

Uachtaráin, and the American Ambassador's residence, where they are less disturbed by human activity.

Both the red and the grey squirrel are associated with Phoenix Park, but by the turn of the millennium few if any red squirrels were extant in the park. The first recorded sighting of the more aggressive grey squirrel was in Áras an Uachtaráin in 1978. The last recorded sighting of the red squirrel was on St Patrick's Day in 1987, according to park management. Unlike the fox, the badger and rabbit who burrow beneath the ground, a squirrel's home, or drey, is usually built in the smaller branches high up in the trees, for safety. It is made of twigs, moss, grass and other vegetation.

While rabbits are widespread in the park, the Irish hare has disappeared from Phoenix Park. Where once it was a feature of a summer's day in the long meadow grasses of the Fifteen Acres, when it would pop up to look about and bound off, it is no longer to be seen. One reason suggested for its disappearance is the practice of allowing dogs to run loose in the park. While the vast majority of canines are trained to behave, some clearly do not. Perhaps the park hare met a sad fate from attacking dogs. Indeed, some fourteen deer were found mortally wounded through 2005 with puncture wounds to their necks, suggesting canine attack of some sort. (We look at the deer herd in the next chapter.)

Another killer, the Irish stoat, often mistakenly called a weasel, can be found in the park. Stoats are known for their enormous curiosity and ferocity. They will kill rabbits, mice and birds and take eggs.

Bats are present in the park as well and make their presence known at nightfall to the discomfort of some strolling humans. The pipistrelle, which weighs only about five grams and is the smallest bat in Ireland, is widespread. Leisler's bat has been observed at the Quarry Lake and in the zoo, and Daubenton's bat has been detected feeding at dusk at the Citadel (or Dog) Pond. It is likely that the long-eared bat is also present in the park.

Pygmy shrews are widespread throughout the park, and can be detected by the squeaking noise they make as they hunt for woodlice, spiders and insects. The wood mouse, also known as the field mouse, can also be found. Inevitably, also present in the park is the brown rat.

Over the years, wild mink have been detected in the park, near the Knockmaroon entrance for the most part, initially. The animal is not native to Ireland, but was introduced in the early 1960s for fur farming. Some escaped to the wild and a population spread. It is a serious threat to other wildlife and will take a wide variety of animals, including fish and rodents. It will also take the eggs and young of water birds.

There are no fish in the Glen Pond for mink or anything else to take, but this does not deter hopeful fishermen arriving from time to time to cast a line in perpetual hope of a bite. There are, however, fish to be found in the Quarry Lake, Citadel Pond and Machine Pond, including pike, perch, roach, bream and carp.

Still, one animal not found in the park anymore or in the whole of Ireland for that matter is the wolf. But it was there, once upon a time. In fact in 1652, it was ordered "that measures be taken for the destruction of wolves in the barony of Castleknock". Luckily, today's authorities take a more wildlife-friendly, conservation-based view.

Times pass and outlooks change and yesterday's problem can be today's nostalgia, but at all levels and throughout the year, wildlife and regeneration continue in Phoenix Park.

11

THE DEER HERD

To some people the Phoenix Park deer are Bambi-like creatures simply there to form a background to family snapshots on a summer's afternoon, or ideal for a quick visit on Christmas Day to thank Rudolph for his generosity and commitment to the work ethic on Christmas Eve. But to others they are a living herd of wild animals with their own rights to the park established over many hundreds of years and through many challenges both to their territory and even to their existence.

Fallow deer have been present in Phoenix Park since the seventeenth century when they were hunted for sport by the gentry of the day. The present-day herd is descended from those deer who were chased for enjoyment and hunted for food.

They are wild animals, even though their habitat is inside a walled park within a European capital city, and they have come to terms with sharing Phoenix Park with man. That relationship has sometimes been a stormy one, such as when there were calls to remove the deer to a special enclosure so that twentieth-century motorists could drive through the park on the way to somewhere else without having deer wandering the roads and precipitating accidents. In fact, their wanderings during the years of the Second World War and pressure on space in general in Phoenix Park saw most of them being officially shot dead.

Fallow deer as a species probably originated in the Mediterranean region about 100,000 years ago, but many perished during the last Ice Age. The survivors migrated from Southern Europe and their dispersal was assisted by man as he ensured his own food supply on his own wanderings. The ancestors of the present-day population of Phoenix Park may have been brought to Ireland in the thirteenth century by the conquering Normans, who had successfully invaded Ireland in 1169.

By 1611, a tempestuous 400 years later, the land now enclosed as Phoenix Park became available to the Crown for the use of its representatives in Ireland. It was suggested then that it would make a fine deer park, and the proposition was looked upon favourably. However, it was not until the arrival in 1662 of James Butler, Duke

Deer are Phoenix Park's living link with history, if not mythology

of Ormond, as Lord Lieutenant, to rule in the King's name, that deer were introduced. Ormond extended the park and stocked it with fallow deer and partridge, but realised that some way of restraining the wild population was required. The park wall was built to prevent the animals from wandering into nearby areas and hunting of the park deer for sport continued.

While in modern times the park is enclosed by a high stone wall with gates provided for both vehicle and pedestrian access, legal penalties now apply for those convicted of harming the deer in any way. Sadly, a number of deer die from injuries and attacks each year, many by dogs who are not leashed by their owners.

The original herd was augmented by new breeding stock that was introduced on a number of occasions during the eighteenth and nineteenth centuries. However, no new deer have been introduced to the Phoenix Park herd since 1904. Interestingly, the animals are clear of most diseases and their gene pool is the subject of study both in Ireland and abroad. The mammal research group within University College Dublin's Department of Zoology in particular has conducted detailed and ongoing research over many years.

There are four varieties of fallow deer in Phoenix Park: black, brown, common and menil. Deer moult and shed their coats in spring and autumn, so varieties in colour and shading are best seen in summer months, when the weather is more conducive to deer-spotting in any case. A gradual selection programme is being followed to ensure menil become the dominant variety in Phoenix Park

While some nice photographs can be taken of grazing deer and the herd will allow humans to approach quite close by, they do have a private life of their own. Strange growling noises emanating from the herd in the glow of an autumn evening can frighten the uninformed and the unwary as they pass through the park's expanse. The menacing sounds come from buck (male) deer on the path to procreation. The noise is designed to impress does (females) with the prowess and virility of the boisterous male, and to help

Bucks will seek dominance before the rut begins in mid-October

give the bellower a favourable position in the herd when the annual propagation period arrives. Top bucks begin vocalising around the third week in September, long before the rut begins in mid-October and before lesser animals in the dominance rank begin to make themselves heard.

Active males don't bother with food during the rutting season, and as a consequence of their fast, and of their amorous efforts, most will lose up to twenty-five per cent of their body weight during the season, according to experts. Short-term vocalisations engaged in by domineering bucks are mostly aimed at other males to dictate their position in the bucking order. However, nothing can go on forever. A top bucking animal's energy wanes and he loses weight and stamina towards the end of the rutting season. It is then that he is likely to encounter challenges from other males who will seek to hop past him in the rank, and by then he may not have the energy to fend off attacks from fresher animals.

In all, fifteen bucks were dominant in the 2005 rut. One buck was observed by UCD students covering 114 does on Hallowe'en 2005 and could have covered up to a total of 200 does when the hours of darkness, after the observers had left the field, were taken into account, according to experts.

The top bucks are tranquillised, weighed and examined before the rut and again afterwards for herd records. These bucks will have a harem of willing does to look after during the rutting season, but contrary to some reports, they do not round up their chosen does. In fact it is the does that choose their favoured buck.

The most dominant bucks will accomplish up to eighty per cent of all matings during a rutting season, gifting a natural strength and health to the offspring. Unfortunately for the weaker males, this can result in them never mating at all, which hardly seems fair to the shy and retiring buck who may have a lot to give. However, when the dominant older males are finished and have returned to the eastern end of the Fifteen Acres and the male herd, younger healthy bucks have a chance at copulating with remaining does, if the doe is receptive.

Gestation takes thirty-three weeks and a single fawn weighing up to four kilogrammes is born in the summer of the following year. Fawns are born in June or July for the most part and lie hidden in long grass where they are dropped by their mothers until they gain strength. Many are to be found in uncut meadow grass on Fifteen Acres. During the birthing weeks, warning signs are erected by park staff, particularly asking dog-owners to keep their animals on a leash. Fawns are most vulnerable to attack from dogs and foxes in their early days.

They can also be distressed by well-meaning humans who come across the curled-up animal and wrongly conclude that the mother has abandoned the baby. Concerned citizens have been known to pick up fawns and stagger off seeking help for the young animal, whose last need is the ministrations of a well-meaning rescuer. The mother is always close by and will return to feed the fawn, left

Fawns are tagged shortly after birth for identification

to her own devices. Young deer are in fact safer in high nettles or in overgrown places where they are mostly hidden from sight until they can fend for themselves, however tentatively.

Some 200 fawns can be born each year in Phoenix Park. And as part of the continuing study of the herd, some hair and nail clippings are taken from the newborn animal for DNA samples, for official records, and to be used in the ongoing study of the herd by the UCD group.

Fawns are colour-tagged shortly after birth and allocated an individual identification number. A different colour tag is used each year, so it is possible to tell the age and individuality of a tagged animal as it travels through its life cycle in Phoenix Park.

Sometimes, if rangers see children out walking in the park with their parents in the vicinity of a find of a new fawn, the rangers may ask the child its name, and duly "christen" the newly born with the same name, which is then entered on the records. The child is told the identification number of the deer and can watch for it in later years. Deerkeeper Don Doran said: "It gets the child interested in nature and it's nice for them to follow the deer later in life." Wildlife studies are now part of the school curriculum and an entry on the deer herd from Mount Sackville students beside the park won an award at the 2005 Young Scientists Competition.

Tagging of the newly born fawns began in 1961, and at any given time there can be twenty years of animals in the park. Tags assist in long-distance identification of individual members of the herd by park workers, who can observe the animals through powerful binoculars without unnecessarily disturbing their habitat.

Normal practice in the case of an injured deer is to observe the progress of the injury, and to make a decision on whether to put down the deer if the injury becomes sufficiently serious. Dead deer are usually buried in the park itself, according to strict protocols. Deer are safely shot in the chest from a distance with a .243 deer hunting rifle using a telescopic sight. DNA forms an increasing part of the study of the herd and when an animal is killed in a road kill, for instance, the ear and its tag are removed from the dead animal for subsequent study.

Healthy fallow deer eat grass and herbs, but also like to eat the bark of old trees. While deer can be plainly seen in their usual grazing grounds, a good indicator of their presence in a particular area is a browse line on nearby trees where hungry animals may have fed on shoots of trees. Deer tracks, called tslots, are long, slender and tapered, and are often read by students of the herd for indication of its activity. Droppings also provide evidence of their presence in a particular area.

Fallow deer are social animals and are usually to be found in large groups in open grassland. The herd is normally situated on the 200-acre flat meadow area known as the Fifteen Acres, and in the woodland of Oldtown Wood on its northern perimeter. Males and females live apart for most of the year except during the breeding season when the bucks compete for dominance and access to does. The buck herd is normally to be found during the day near the

Grazing deer are a common site on the park's grasslands

football and hurling pitches, while the females may be found not too far away in the area broadly between the perimeter walls of the American Ambassador's residence and St Mary's Hospital and within site of the Papal Cross.

Young bucks join the male herd during their second or third year of life, having lived with their mother's herd until then. Most young bucks wait four or five years until they are able to compete on a level footing with older more established males in the breeding stakes. Females, for their part, can breed at eighteen months of age, but do not usually do so until they have reached two years of age. Male deer may live to be twelve years of age in Phoenix Park, while a female could live to be twenty years of age. The oldest recorded male died of old age in summer 2004 at fourteen years of age. His skeleton was placed on exhibition in the mammal study unit in UCD. Few detailed records were kept in earlier times, so it is possible that some males lived longer.

Herd numbers have fluctuated over the centuries. The herd has the capacity to double its numbers every five years, if unchecked.

At one time, the deer population totalled more than 1,200 animals. At other times, during the Second World War for instance, just thirty-eight animals constituted the herd, following the 1942 cull.

During the Second World War, local allotment holders who were growing vegetables on allocated spaces on the Fifteen Acres and the polo grounds demanded action when deer began to eat the holders' produce. Their depredation caused questions to be asked in Dáil Éireann of the Minister for Finance on 30 June 1942. However, Finance Minister O'Ceallaigh rejected opposition calls for more fencing to be installed to prevent access by deer and summer grazing cattle. Nonetheless, a severe cull of the herd ordered in 1942 brought more questions in the Dáil on 15 October. The herd had grown by this time to between 800 and 850 animals and it was decided to reduce it to fewer than forty animals, which was considered adequate as a nucleus for the future.

The deer were rounded up and were shot over a five-month period, through an exceptionally harsh winter. Strangely, given that there was a war on, little interest was shown in Dublin in the fresh venison now available from Phoenix Park. The dead animals were exported to Britain where the wartime controlled price for venison on first hand sale for unskinned carcasses was eight pence per pound. The cull was the subject of heated exchanges in the Dáil, over the method by which the contractor was appointed. Hugo Victor Flinn TD, the Parliamentary Secretary to the Minister for Finance, told the opposition that the contractor, the Associated Merchandise Company, of Holles Place, Dublin, was in fact the only one to show interest in the task.

Herd numbers recovered after this most severe winter cull and by November 1974, on the occasion of an annual count, the herd had increased once more to 300.

In the 1980s an average of some thirty-seven deer were being killed in the park each year as commuter motor traffic increased through the park. Others died at the jaws of dogs, some were injured as a result of being shot by pellet guns and some even met their deaths at the hands of poachers with crossbows.

By 1996, there were almost 1,000 animals in the herd once more. A dangerous situation arose as a consequence, as deer followed traditional paths across the park, and the areas surrounding Phoenix Park saw an upsurge in house building development as Dublin housing demand spread into the suburbs. Heavy commuter use of the park's roads and the death of at least two animals every week in collisions with motor vehicles provoked serious concerns.

Many animals endured painful deaths following traffic accidents on those occasions when death was not immediate. Most accidents involving deer happen in the long winter hours of darkness when wandering animals cross the roads and meet hurrying motorists, mostly on the four kilometres of main road on Chesterfield Avenue between Castleknock and Parkgate Street Gates.

In the late 1990s, a cull was conducted to reduce herd numbers, and measures were taken to reduce and slow the flow of commuter traffic through the park at peak times. However, a proposal for a specially enclosed deer area, with the herd being corralled inside so that motor traffic could flow more easily, was rejected by park management as being unsuitable. The deer's natural habitat is woodland edge, and enclosure is not necessarily the best solution to problems caused by the confluence of wildlife and modern commuting society. The open spaces of Phoenix Park are ideal as far as vegetation and habitat are concerned for the free wandering of a healthy and active deer herd.

While suggestions of corralling the herd is rejected as impractical, there are times when the herd itself is prevented from entering an area. Once the annual letting of grazing for cattle was discontinued in Phoenix Park in 1983, the deer herd quickly took over the newly available grasslands of the park. However, one area where they were prevented from grazing was the new plantation near to the Furry Glen where a high deer fence was erected in the 1990s to keep the animals out while new trees grew to strength.

While most dangers facing the herd come from within the park, by 2001 the herd faced a different danger. A number of cases of foot-and-mouth disease were discovered amongst sheep herds in Ireland and travel restrictions were imposed across the country. The Irish Deer Society called, in vain as it happened, for the complete closure of Phoenix Park as a precaution against the possible spread of foot-and-mouth disease to the deer there. The Leinster branch of the society objected to allowing motor traffic through the park at all. It said Phoenix Park was a huge farm with 400 to 500 fallow deer and should be treated like any other farm. However, Dúchas, the Heritage Service, which had responsibility for the park at the time, said it allowed cars through on veterinary advice from the Department of Agriculture. In the event, the outbreak was contained nationally and did not spread to Phoenix Park.

However, once that threat passed, by 2004, some fifty deer were being killed in collisions with motorists, at a rate of almost one a week; admittedly a figure half of the accident rate in 1996, before widespread traffic control measures came into force, but nonetheless a horrific toll on the herd.

By 2005, the herd had grown to some 800 animals once more and a major reduction was ordered by the Office of Public Works, which once more had taken over responsibility for management of Phoenix Park. Some 350 animals were to be killed to reduce the herd to a manageable size of 450 animals once more. A deer population of this size was regarded as the maximum carrying capacity of the park, according to the OPW. The intent of the cull was to have a slimmer more manageable herd within the confines of the park. The cull will be carried out over a number of years taking into account the number of healthy or infirm specimens there are alive from each year of birth. No year will be put at risk through over-selection of particular animals, according to park management.

The husbandry and history of the herd reflects the history of Phoenix Park and of Dublin and of Ireland itself, as both internal and external events touch the animals while they graze and wander and live and love in the relatively tranquil surroundings of Phoenix Park, as the herd has done for hundreds of years, and will continue to do so for many years to come.

12

SELF-GUIDED TRAILS

Phoenix Park has a great many walking paths for the leisure walker to explore. Many tracks take off through the long grass and wander along through meadow grasses to nowhere in particular. None are far from a road or a bus route or a car park, yet some lead to quiet secluded parts of the park where the only sound is of rustling in the undergrowth as park life continues, or begins, as ever.

Phoenix Park is a man-made landscape, and is not an area of wild nature. Almost every part of it looks as it does now because of the design and hand of man. The area at Furry Glen and beside Knockmaroon Gates is a quarter designated for the preservation of wildlife and as such will be touched as little as possible by man.

FURRY GLEN NATURE TRAIL

About 60 minutes' leisurely walking with strong footwear

When the Furry Glen Nature Trail was laid out some years ago, it was designed to fill a leisurely hour's walk. The trail is unmarked now, though the OPW has said the markers will be replaced and the trail is outlined on official maps. In some places a mouldering wooden post will still point the way with an arrow to where sister posts have long since given up the ghost. The old trail may be followed by walking north from the old disused circular information centre beside the Knockmaroon Gate car park along a narrow tarmac path, across the closed road and up to a slightly higher level where a wood of birch trees is criss-crossed by paths worn by many walking feet over years.

A stone plaque a short distance into the wood declares that the trees were planted in 1898. Turning right, the walker will eventually come to the steps above the waters of the Glen Pond. Many species of deciduous trees, including oak, ash, elm, sycamore, beech and chestnut are planted in the area of the Glen Pond. Some specimens are susceptible to woodland deteriorations, many of them caused by fungi. The fungus grows first as a parasite on the living trees, but continues to grow on the dead wood even after it has killed the living tree. On either side of the paths through the woodland can be seen fungi growing out of dead tree trunks.

The Furry Glen is now designated as a "wilderness" or wildlife conservation area

In keeping with the policy of allowing nature to take its course in the wilderness area, creeping ivy can be seen slowly assuming the shape of a large sycamore, for instance, as it colonises the parent tree until there is a spectacular ivy tree growing high above the woodland floor.

Different trees in woodland are obvious to all, but the variety of grasses in grassland may escape casual observation, according to an official guide to the old nature trail. The leaves are difficult to distinguish, but the "spikes" of grass flowers are distinct. The narrow, one-sided spike of dog's-tail, wedge-shaped clusters of cocksfoot, the spike of rye grass with spikelets in two regular rows, the compact yellowish spike of vernal grass, and the soft spreading head of Yorkshire fog are common grasses that are easy to recognise, according to the guide.

While the higher part of the wilderness area showcases grassland and woodland, a lower area is dominated by the water feature of the Glen Pond. Wooden steps have been cut into the steep embankment to allow a winding walk down to the water's edge from the dense woodland above.

The small lake known as Glen Pond is an artificial lake, dammed by a bank on which the road across the glen is built. The tarmac road has been closed to motor traffic for years to preserve the tranquillity of the Glen. The corner on the northern side of the pond where the road turns at an angle away from the water was in the 1940s the scene of crossroad dancing when locals gathered there for céilís. Music has long since faded in the glen and the visitor is more likely to hear birdsong and flapping wings than a happy accordion launching into yet another set of an evening.

The pond proper is a breeding-place in spring for coots, the black water-birds with white foreheads and bills that live there all year round. Moorhen and other birds may be seen scudding across the water as well. Vegetation around the edge is typical of a transition from dry land to deep water with some iris growing at the edge; there is reed grass growing further in, and water lilies and pondweed float on the surface farthest from the bank.

Steps have been provided on the northern side of the glen for access to the meadowland of Fifteen Acres above. Gorse used to grow in abundance on the steep slope of the valley here where cattle and deer cannot easily graze. Once established, gorse is fairly resistant to grazing animals because of its sharp spines. In high summer, pods of gorse, or furze, may be heard bursting and scattering seed, which are distributed farther by busy ants as they go about their undisturbed business at ground level. The Furry Glen may be named after the furze in the glen.

Rising up from the glen by more wooden steps, walkers meet the waving meadow of the Fifteen Acres across the road, stretching towards the city in the distance. An eighteenth-century walker travelling through the western extremity of the grasslands near the Glen Pond would have encountered an area laid out as a cultivated garden on Fifteen Acres, which lent its name to the area. The enclosure is long gone but the name remains, although the Fifteen Acres is some 200 acres in size by now.

Walking across Fifteen Acres and veering left towards a roundel of oak trees, members of the park's own wild deer herd may be seen. The ancestors of these deer were introduced to the park in 1662. The oak wood was planted in 1897 and the walker will see how the woods in a cultivated park are different from natural woodlands. In this plantation there are no other trees apart from oak, whereas most natural woods have several tree species, even if one is predominant. In natural woodland, as the wilderness area to the south was planned to be, trees of all ages and sizes grow as saplings develop in the spaces left by dead trees.

Crossing the tarmac road at the nearby crossroads walkers will meet a downward path leading back down to the pond level and following it come to a junction on the floor of the glen. The junction, if taken to the left returns to the water's edge, if taken to the right leads up to Baker's Well, sometimes referred to as St Brigid's Well by locals, which feeds into the Glen Pond. Above the well is the road which leads back to Knockmaroon Gate to the left and to the car park once more.

A shorter version of the walk can be taken that just leads down to the level of the Glen Pond and back up to the Knockmaroon Gate.

HERITAGE TRAIL: CHESTERFIELD AVENUE FROM CASTLEKNOCK GATE

About 45 minutes' leisurely walking

Chesterfield Avenue is the great avenue of Phoenix Park and is laid out to run straight all the way between Parkgate Street entrance on the city side and Castleknock Gate at the western extremity. The avenue is four kilometres long and named for Lord Chesterfield who, in 1745, opened what was a royal deer park to the people.

A misty morning on Chesterfield Avenue

Its present alignment is bordered by lines of lime, beech and horse chestnut dating from 1840 when landscape designer Decimus Burton laid out the road to be a "grand avenue".

While paths for walking and cycling are provided on either side of the park's main road, the OPW has laid out a series of hip-high information plaques on the southern side of the road as a self-guiding heritage trail, starting at the Castleknock Gate. The first sign displays an engraved map of Phoenix Park and marks the beginning of the trail proper along Chesterfield Avenue.

The second marker records the fact that Castleknock Lodge and Gate was designed by Burton in 1837 at a cost of £840 and replaced a much larger lodge and outhouses of earlier times. In fact, Burton's concepts play a large part in the lay-out of Phoenix Park where no two lodges are built to the same design.

The next marker notes that the park is enclosed by a random rubble stone wall some eleven kilometres long and four metres high. Construction of the wall started in 1671 but by 1672 large parts of it had fallen down such was the poor workmanship of the contractor. It was subsequently rebuilt by a different contractor, to better effect. The wall is a protected structure and nothing may be built against it, or attached to it, on the inside or the outside perimeter.

Along the path between the lines of mature trees may be seen examples of some Phoenix Park tree guards. The guards protect young trees from grazing animals and fallow deer in particular. The guards range from the traditional free-standing strap type to a modern expanded metal one.

Farmleigh Clock Tower

Phoenix Park does not exist in isolation and the neighbouring Farmleigh clock tower, dating from 1880, may be glimpsed between the trees, although it is outside the park proper. Farmleigh was bought for the State in 1999 and its official entrance is now off nearby White's Road.

Mountjoy Cross

The first major crossroads on Chesterfield Avenue on the way towards the city is to be re-designed and a roundabout installed as part of park management. It is called after the nearby and former Mountjoy Barracks, in turn named for Lord Mountjoy whose home it was. It is now the home of Ordnance Survey Ireland. The junction is a pivotal part of the annual motor races and is the scene of more than one spin-out during the races. Two ponds are located near to Mountjoy Cross: the Machine Pond on the north side into which a grass-cutting machine fell and was never seen again, so deep is the pond, or so the story goes; and Quarry Pond on the southern side.

Quarry Pond

This was once a quarry and formerly stored water for various parts of the park. Phoenix Park is on a plateau and water is pumped upwards to many of the dwellings. An island sits in the middle of the old quarry's water and it is sometimes called the Island Pond.

The Machine Pond

Looking north across the road, the wide grass expanse of Whitefields runs to Ashtown Gate in the distance. The flat grasslands are used as a concert site and as a pit area for the annual motor races.

Slí na Sláinte

Along the way on both sides of Chesterfield Avenue, some colourful marker buoys stand at a distance of one kilometre apart. They are part of an eight-kilometre Irish Heart Foundation "Slí na Sláinte" health initiative to encourage people to walk for pleasure and for good health. The walk takes in four kilometres on one side of the road and four kilometres back on the other side. The uprights were specially designed to complement the existing bollards of Phoenix Park. Stone ordnance bench markers and metal marker bollards and Victorian handrails may be seen along Chesterfield Avenue.

Gas Lights

Gas lights, the traditional form of park illumination, were first installed along Chesterfield Avenue by the Hibernian Gas Company in 1859 and were fully refurbished in 1987. Though now automated, the early installations had to be lit each evening by a lamplighter. The rear entrance to the United States Ambassador's residence is served by a narrow access road running behind this marker.

Ashtown Demesne

A lodge to the north of Chesterfield Avenue marks the front entrance to Ashtown demesne which includes Ashtown Castle, now restored and open as Phoenix Park Visitor Centre. A plaque draws attention to a clump of ancient oaks standing on the north side of the road.

Phoenix Column

The Phoenix Column was erected in 1747 on the opening of the park to the public. The bird on top is the Phoenix, a mythical bird that rises from its own ashes. The column is now the centrepiece of a large roundabout which slows traffic and allows some pedestrian access from one side of the road to the other. There are no designated pedestrian crossings in Phoenix Park, an omission felt keenly by wheelchair users and pram walkers when commuter traffic is at its height.

Áras an Uachtaráin Phoenix Entrance

Design of the imposing entrance to Áras an Uachtaráin, home of the Irish President, is attributed to Burton. There were two other entrances to the presidential enclosure, one called the City Gate, the other the Laundry Gate. The latter remains as a trade entrance off the Back Road but while the gate and its lodge remain intact, the land behind City Gate is now part of Dublin Zoo.

Deerfield

The house now known as Deerfield was originally built in 1776 by Sir John Blaquiere, Bailiff of Phoenix Park. Its entrance gates are to be seen to the south of the Phoenix Column roundabout. It is the home of the serving Ambassador of the United States of America.

George Bernard Shaw Grove

East of the Phoenix roundabout and south of the road were planted some ninety-three trees in the Shaw Plantation in 1992 with funds raised on behalf of the Dublin Shaw Society. A tree was planted for each year of Shaw's life. A plaque marks the spot as the trail moves towards the busier end of Chesterfield Avenue.

The entrance gates to Deerfield, Residence of the US Ambassador

Papal Cross

From the main road can also be seen the Papal Cross on Fifteen Acres. It was part of the altar for the mass celebrated by Pope John Paul II before a million and a quarter people in 1979. Ceremonies for the Eucharistic Congress in 1932 and Catholic Emancipation centenary celebrations in 1929 also took place in this part of the park.

Polo Grounds and Pavilion

The All-Ireland Polo Club, the second oldest polo club in the world, was formed in Carlow in 1837. By 1847, the first game was played in this part of the park, formerly known as the Nine Acres, and games continue at weekends, in season, on the northern side of Chesterfield Avenue.

Garda Athletic Grounds

A pavilion marks the first of the spaces allotted to sports off the southern side of Chesterfield Avenue. The building is the clubhouse for the Garda Athletic Grounds and beyond that lie changing rooms for the adjacent much-used camogie pitches.

Cricket Grounds

There are two cricket clubs in the park, Phoenix and Civil Service. There were some twenty cricket grounds in Phoenix Park in the early 1900s, including a public pitch on the Fifteen Acres, where anybody could book space to play. Interest in the game declined after independence was achieved and with the rise in popularity of soccer and the GAA throughout the country.

Dog Pond or Citadel Pond

A bomb was dropped near the Citadel Pond by a German bomber on the night of Saturday 31 May 1941. The occupants of the adjacent pump house escaped injury, but the house had to be demolished. The Citadel Pond, also known as the Dog Pond, is sometimes used for floating model and toy boats. Dog walkers also encourage their charges to fetch thrown objects from the water. Unlike this pond, other ponds in the park are maintained mainly as features of the park landscape.

Dublin Zoo

Dublin Zoo was established in 1831 when the Lord Lieutenant let the use of a portion of the park then known as The Garden to the Zoological Society, which had been recently established, for the establishment of a menagerie. It opened with a single boar as the attraction. Today it is a national attraction enjoyed by many thousands of visitors. There have been three entrances since the Gardens opened to the public and all may still be seen on Zoo Road beside one another.

Kiosk Tea Rooms

The annual report of the Commissioner of Public Works for 1895/1896 records the presence of a refreshment kiosk with a verandah and enclosure. The tearooms are operated by lessees and have remained popular for refreshments for more than a century. The lease in recent years was joined with the lease for the Fionn Uisce restaurant in the Visitor Centre up the road, creating obvious synergies between the two facilities.

People's Flower Gardens

In 1864, the People's Flower Gardens were laid out beside the park's main gates and opposite the newly completed Wellington monument. Its lake is the lower of three in this part of the park. Another in Dublin Zoo is the middle lake and an upper stretch of water in Áras an Uachtaráin is the upper lake, also known as the Fish Pond,

The bandstand in The Hollow

much of which is now incorporated into Dublin Zoo's African Plains. The gardens are a fine example of formal Victorian horticulture.

Wellington Monument

The imposing Wellington Monument commemorates the Dublin-born Iron Duke's victory at Waterloo against Napoleon in 1815. At sixty-seven metres high, it was second in height as an obelisk only to the Washington Memorial's 169 metres for many years. The Dublin Spire on O'Connell Street is 120 metres high and was completed in 2003.

The final Slí na Sláinte marker lies some metres to the east of Wellington and marks the end of the Heritage Trail.

WALKING IN A CIRCLE

About 60 minutes' comfortable walking

A circular walk may be undertaken from the car park at the Papal Cross by walking south towards St Mary's Hospital, around by Chapelizod and the Furry Glen, across to Mountjoy Cross, east to Phoenix roundabout and back to the Papal Cross.

Heading south on the Acres Road towards the Dublin mountains in the distance, the relative height of Phoenix Park above the Liffey Valley can be gauged by the clear view across the south city to the hills beyond.

On the left is the top end of Khyber Road, now closed to through traffic, but which passes below Magazine Hill at its further extremity on its way to Islandbridge Gate. The Pump Wood divides the Khyber Road from the Acres Road and was the location for the last mound of turf to be removed in the 1960s left over from the huge turf banks held in a massive fuel dump during the Second World War.

A little further on are the designated playing pitches for soccer and Gaelic games. Mature trees surrounding the dressing room area when seen from a distance seem to be painted into the landscape.

The Magazine Fort can be seen to the east end of the pitches. The Powder Magazine was built in 1735 on St Thomas' Hill where the original Phoenix House stood. It held munitions for the Dublin garrisons. The star fort was a military store until it was handed back to the OPW by the Department of Defence in 1988. It is surrounded by a dry ditch and originally included a drawbridge for the protection of its defenders.

St Mary's Hospital

The hospital is the former Hibernian Military Academy which for 150 years up to 1922 cared for the orphaned or abandoned children of soldiers who served in the British army. The foundation stone was laid in 1786. St Mary's was for a while an Irish military hospital and then a tuberculosis sanatorium. It is currently in use as a hospital.

Stone steps lead down the hill beside the hospital's main entrance and walkers arrive on the now-closed St Mary's Road to turn west or right towards the Furry Glen.

Chapelizod Gate

At the foot of the slope below the hospital can be seen Chapelizod Gate and Lodge, designed by Decimus Burton. He designed the gate and entrance to frame the Hibernian Academy atop the hill as the visitor entered the park.

Cromlech

A sign near the Cheshire Home to the west of St Mary's Hospital indicates where an early Bronze Age cromlech is to be found on the top of the hill on the right. Knockmary burial mound was excavated in 1838. A stone slab is all that is to be seen on the eastern side of the park ranger's lodge.

Chapelizod Turnstile

The turnstile at Chapelizod's Park Lane at the foot of Knockmary Hill was the original entrance to Phoenix Park from Chapelizod. Inspection will show three piers in the wall which allowed for separate vehicular entrance as well as for pedestrian access. It is now pedestrian-only.

St Lawrence's Church

Further west along the road, and built outside the park walls but clearly visible from within, the church in its present form was built in 1830. A church existed on the site from the thirteenth century and the square tower is older than the rest of the building. It is believed to be the site of Iosolde's chapel, of Tristan and Iosolde fame, whence Chapelizod derives its name. The graveyard beside the church featured in ghost stories of Sheridan Le Fanu, who as a boy lived in the Hibernian Academy with his family while his father served as chaplain there.

Stewart's Hospital, Palmerstown

In the distance across the Liffey Valley at Palmerstown can be seen the former home of the Earl of Donoughmore. It was purchased in 1872 as an institution for the mentally handicapped. It continues to serve the same purpose today as Stewart's Hospital. It is called after Sir Henry Stewart who handed over his own private asylum at Lucan Spa to a committee of the new institution in 1869.

The Furry Glen

One of the most scenic and natural areas in the park. Formerly known as the Hawthorn or Fairy Glen because of the numerous hawthorns that bloomed in May and June in the area, not to mention the fairies who may have lived there as well. It may also have derived its name from the furze or gorse which grows abundantly. The Glen in recent years has formed the centrepiece for a wild section of the park where wildlife is protected.

Woodland Path

Walkers may step across the road to follow a woodland path beside the twisting Upper Glen Road. A carpark has been provided in this area since the lower Glen Road was closed to traffic some years ago. The path continues to a confluence of Knockmaroon Road on the left, the Ordnance Survey Road ahead and Furze Road to the right. The latter is also closed to through traffic and picnic benches have been provided on the roadside on the perimeter of Oldtown Wood.

Rose Cottage

The walk continues through the crossroads. A continuous path has been laid to facilitate walkers moving along past a public-sponsored plantation of trees, planted to replace decaying trees in Oldtown Wood, and past the hexagonal Rose Cottage, another of the park's unique lodges.

Ordnance Survey

The Ordnance Survey on the left was originally the residence of Luke Gardiner, later Lord Mountjoy. In 1812, the residence was converted to be Mountjoy Cavalry Barracks. It later housed the mounted escort to the Lord Lieutenant who lived where Áras an Uachtaráin is now. Ordnance Survey Ireland took up residence in 1824. The footpath running across to Furze Road opposite the Survey is called Tinkler's Path, according to local maps, and can be a dry shortcut to the picnic area.

Ponds

Past the Ordnance Survey on the right is the Island or Quarry Pond and straight ahead on the corner of Chesterfield Avenue is the Machine Pond.

Chesterfield Avenue

A turn to the right, or to the east and the city, faces the walker in the correct direction to pick up the Chesterfield Avenue trail (above) on the way back to the Phoenix Column and the nearby carpark at the Papal Cross once more.

AROUND THE WALL FROM CASTLEKNOCK TO CASTLEKNOCK

About two hours' walking, using stout footwear

It is possible to walk along the perimeter wall from Castleknock gate in either direction and believe the motor car has not yet been invented. The well-trodden path is criss-crossed with roots of trees planted hundreds of years ago which tower above the modern walker. It is a remote area and best walked in company, for the most part, since in centuries past it was notorious for its complement of highwaymen and thieves, and who knows what miscreants one may happen upon in a modern setting.

Heading north from Castleknock Gate at the start of the eleven-kilometre walk, an example of a sunken fence may be seen not far into the trees; Decimus Burton designed these sunken parameters to allow a clear view across the parkland. Many plantations of trees in this area are in roundel patterns where the trees are of the same species, age and height for the most part.

Further along the wall the Whitefields works enclosure may be seen. The enclosure is the park's administration, work and storage areas. The vehicular entrance to Whitefields is some ten minutes' walk from Castleknock Gate, if the meandering path through the trees is followed. Inside the gate may be seen the Park Superintendent's Lodge. Once the Bailiff's Lodge, it was designed by Jacob Owen in 1832.

Another five minutes' walk and the rambler meets Ashtown Gate Lodge, which is really three lodges clustered around the gate. In addition to the main lodge, there is Bessborough Lodge East which, along with Bessborough Lodge West, formed Bessborough police barracks in times past. Designed by Burton as barracks and accommodation for police, it was completed in 1848.

Just before the lodges are met a large concrete base marks the spot where once cattle destined for summer grazing in the park were assembled, tagged and branded. A disused concrete loading platform is extant here, though its railings have withered away. Up to 1,000 cattle were processed through here as they came and left the park each year.

Further along the way lies Phoenix Park School, still in use as a school, and beside it the Swiss cottage design of the Concrete Lodge.

The wall along the Back Road is interesting for having a number of pedestrian turnstiles as well as entrances for motor traffic. The first stile is at the Hole in the Wall pub on Blackhorse Avenue where a sign informs that the hostelry dates from 1651, though it is outside the park perimeter.

Inside the park and across the road is Ratra House, the headquarters of the Civil Defence and the retirement home from 1949 of Douglas Hyde, the first President of Ireland.

Opposite the second turnstile is the 200-year-old Buggy's Lodge beside the back entrance to Áras an Uachtaráin.

It was proposed in the 1830s to relocate the nearby Cabra Gate and Lodge to partially close the Back Road, but the proposal never materialised. The Back Road continues to be used by heavy commuter traffic into the twenty-first century.

An old laundry located beside the trade entrance to Áras an Uachtaráin close at hand was used for many years as Cabra Garda station, before a new station was built on the nearby Navan Road. The Laundry Lodge dates from 1895 and was occupied by the chief steward of the Vice Regal Lodge.

A third turnstile is located opposite to the new works entrance to the extended Dublin Zoo. A fourth stile and vehicular gates lead out of the park to Blackhorse Avenue and to a military graveyard across the road. The vehicular gates are kept closed but were opened and widened during the papal visit of 1979 to facilitate movement.

Spa Road used to mark the delineation between the Vice Regal Lodge and Dublin Zoo, but expansion of the Zoo in the 1990s past the road saw the roadway being narrowed to preclude motor traffic. Pedestrians and cyclists may still use the narrowed carriageway.

Further along the wall of the park is the back entrance to McKee military barracks located just before the imposing two-storey building at the Garda Depot which houses a Garda officers' club. The building dates from 1863 and is the design of Benjamin Woodward. The large Garda Headquarters was once the Garda training depot and before that was home to the RIC's training depot. Single men's quarters were provided beside the nearby park gate.

The North Circular Road Gate and Lodge marks the turning point of the wall as it carries on in an easterly direction skirting the People's Flower Gardens and the Defence Forces Headquarters to emerge at Parkgate Street and Chesterfield Avenue after about an hour's walking.

A ruined building on the southern side of Chesterfield Avenue inside Parkgate Street gate was a DMP police barracks. It was later used by the new force of the Garda Síochána as a sub-station to Cabra station on the Back Road. It closed down in the 1930s.

Beside the ruins, the park's own greenhouses are located in a secluded corner known as the Klondike, after the area of Canada where a gold rush took place in 1897. Ever since they were built in the late nineteenth century, the glasshouses have been used for the growing of plants for the People's Flower Gardens and other official requirements.

A stone tablet indicates that evergreen oaks growing nearby were donated in 1904 by Sir Arthur Edward Guinness who presented some 800 specimens that were grown from seed collected in 1887.

Heading back up Chesterfield Avenue the walker comes to the Wellington Monument on the left. Nearby stone steps lead down to a number of turnstiles at Islandbridge. In the distance at the opposite height above the Liffey Valley can be seen the Royal Hospital Kilmainham, now the home of the Irish Museum of Modern Art. It once marked the southern boundary of Phoenix Park lands. The Irish National War Memorial at Islandbridge can also be seen across the river from this vantage point.

Lower down the hill stands Burton's Islandbridge vehicular gate. A viewing spot opposite the gate was used by artists to paint views of the Liffey as it flows towards the city. The famous Malton images were painted from here at the end of the eighteenth century.

The wall rises once more to the Corkscrew or Military Road and past the old Military magazine on St Thomas's Hill. The magazine stands on the site of the original Phoenix House. It is no longer used for military purposes.

The Timekeeper's or Fort Lodge is on this road and was the home of the Assistant Park Superintendent. While in modern times the nearby Deer Lodge is used to house park constables and their families, the Deer Lodge was once home to the park's official Deerkeeper.

The exterior of the refurbished football pavilions located in close proximity to the lodges has been preserved for historical reasons in a major re-fit of the changing rooms.

The sloping area inside the perimeter wall between Islandbridge and Chapelizod, below the Corkscrew Road, was mooted to be a suitable site for a large flower bed, under allotments, during the debate on the Phoenix Park Bill in 1925, but the proposal came to nothing.

Past this area, which is currently under grassland, Chapelizod Gate and Lodge were designed by Burton to replace an older Chapelizod entrance at nearby Park Lane. The vehicular entrance was moved so that people entering the park could see the Hibernian Academy, now St Mary's Hospital, stretching across the ridge in front of them. An old quarry beside the gates has been used for many years as a landfill for material removed from elsewhere in the park.

The park wall runs along to Park Lane turnstile and on up a slope to meet the Glen Road once more. A signposted path leads from the turnstile to the top of Knockmary Hill where a cromlech is to be found beside the park ranger's lodge.

Private pedestrian gates set into the wall along the path here hark back to past privilege for adjoining landowners. The road forks soon afterwards with the lower Glen Road following the line of the park wall and the Upper Road skirting the Furry Glen.

The Lower Glen Road crosses the glen with the pond on one side and a ravine on the other, which are both part of the wilderness area of Phoenix Park's development and management. The road swings around on its way to Knockmaroon Gates and passes another private pedestrian entrance set into the wall. It gives access to a property once owned by the Guinness family.

Knockmaroon Gates, also designed by Burton, were once exit points for leisure drives from the city through Phoenix Park to the rural Strawberry Beds. It features two sets of vehicular entrances. However the entrance leading directly to Furry Glen has been closed for many years as the glen area was developed into a wilderness protection area.

Nearby, Mount Sackville Convent also has a private pedestrian entrance into Phoenix Park. It was once the home of Lord George Sackville. From 1775 to 1782 he was the British Secretary of State for America before the United States came into being.

A well-worn path runs along beside the wall here and will eventually meet the tarmac road at White's Gate and the entrance to Farmleigh, having skirted the perimeter of Ordnance Survey. The path is once more through a quiet and remote area and is pitted with the roots of trees planted many hundreds of years ago, making for an interesting walk underfoot.

The vehicular entrance at White's Gate was closed in the 1990s in an attempt to introduce traffic control to the western side of the park, which had seen huge increases in commuter traffic as

Dublin developed around Phoenix Park. A pedestrian gate allows for walkers to pass through and out of the park.

The path beside the wall resumes after White's Gate Lodge is passed and a short distance on the walker arrives once more at Castleknock Gate having completed an eleven-kilometre circumference of Phoenix Park.

Opening Times and Other Information

Áras an Uachtaráin

Website: http://www.president.ie/
Home of the President of Ireland. Situated off Chesterfied Avenue and accessed off the Phoenix roundabout. Free tours on Saturdays start from Phoenix Park Visitor Centre.

Band Hollow

Amphitheatre near Zoo with a Victorian bandstand where free summer Sunday afternoon concerts are conducted.

Buses and Horses

A horsedrawn carriage service from the Wellington Monument has been suspended. Dublin Bus provides scheduled services to most of the park gates: Routes 25, 26, 66, 67 serve Parkgate Street, Islandbridge and Chapelizod Gates. Routes 37, 38, 39 serve Cabra, Ashtown and Castleknock Gates. Route 10 serves North Circular Road Gate.

Dublin Zoo

Tel: 01 6771425
Website: www.dublinzoo.ie
One of Europe's oldest zoos dating from 1830. Open every day except Christmas Day. Situated near Parkgate Street and North Circular Road Gates.

Farmleigh

Website: www.farmleigh.ie
Farmleigh is the official State guest house and was formerly a private residence of the Guinness family. It is accessed off White's Gate Road. The entrance is a fifteen-minute walk from Castleknock Gate for those accessing the park from that side. The OPW operates a public access programme, which provides an opportunity for the public to enjoy the house and grounds at Farmleigh.

Papal Cross

Situated near Chesterfield Avenue's Phoenix roundabout the area has a carpark and is used by many as a rendezvous point. The forty-one metre high steel cross commemorates the 1979 visit of Pope John Paul II to Phoenix Park when a reported million and a quarter people attended a papal mass.

People's Flower Gardens

A separate flower garden with lake and children's playground situated beside Parkgate Street and North Circular Road Gates. Dating from the late 1800s, the gardens are maintained in the Victorian tradition of horticulture. The gardens have opening and closing times of their own, usually starting at 10.30 am and closing at twilight.

Phoenix Park Visitor Centre

Tel 01 6770095

Interpretive centre with static and audio-visual displays on the park. Restaurant and toilets and car park provided. Free tours of Áras an Uachtaráin leave from here on Saturdays. Access for pedestrians or cars from Phoenix roundabout on Chesterfield Avenue. Dublin Bus Nos. 37, 38 or 39 to Ashtown Gate. Once inside the gate, walk to the T-junction and turn left, walk for about ten minutes until you reach a pathway on the right-hand side to lead you towards the trees and the back gate of Ashtown Castle. Alternatively, use bus No. 10 to North Circular Road Gate; be aware that it's a healthy thirty-minute walk from this gate to the centre.

SPORT

Motor Races

Website: www.motorsportireland.com

Usually held over two days in August on a triangular route centred on Mountjoy Crossroads near Castleknock gate. Access is free.

Polo

Website: www.allirelandpoloclub.com

On polo grounds off Chesterfield Avenue. 1 May to 30 September, Saturday and Sunday, 3.15 pm.

Soccer

On football pitches on Fifteen Acres. Mid-August to mid-May, Sunday, 10.00 am to 2.30 pm and evenings 7.00 pm to 9.00 pm, mid-April to mid-May.

Hurling, Gaelic and Camogie

Played most months to some extent on pitches on Fifteen Acres and on camogie pitches near to the Dog Pond.

Cricket

Civil Service and Phoenix Cricket Clubs play mid-April to mid-September on pitches off Chesterfield Avenue and close to the Dog Pond.

Other Sports

Phoenix Park is used by a great many sports for both collective and singular activities. The best way to find them is to go look and ask locally.

Walks

A number of walks are marked out in the park; see Chapter 12 for details.

FURTHER READING

Publications

As I Was Going Down Sackville Street by Oliver St John Gogarty

A Candle in the Window by Jim Lacey, published by Marino Books

Dignam's Dublin Guide 1891

Down Ratra Road: Fifty Years of Civil Defence in Ireland, published by The Stationery Office

First Class Service: A History of Civil Service Cricket Club, published by CCSS

The Freeman's Journal

Hard Cases: True Stories of Irish Crimes by Gene Kerrigan, 1996

History of Phoenix Park and Visitor's Handbook by J.W. O'Beirne

A History of the County Dublin by Francis Ellington Ball, 1907

History of the Royal Hibernian School edited by G.H. O'Reilly, published by The Genealogical Society of Ireland.

Michael Cusack and the GAA by Marcus de Burca, published by Anvil, 1987

North Dublin City and Environs by Dillon Cosgrave, published by M.H. Gill & Son

Ordnance Survey in Ireland, published by OSI

The Phoenix Park by Kenneth Mac Gowan, published by Kamac Publications

Racing in the Park by Bob Montgomery, published by Dreoilín

The Royal Irish Constabulary by Jim Herlihy, published by Four Courts Press, 1997

Triumph of the Red Devil by Brendan Lynch, published by Portobello Publishing

Up in the Park: Diary of the Wife of the American Ambassador to Ireland, 1977-81 by Elizabeth Shannon, published by Gill & Macmillan

Websites

Áras an Uachtaráin: www.president.ie

BirdWatch Ireland: http://www.birdwatchireland.ie

Bohemians FC: www.bohemians.ie

Civil Defence: www.civildefence.ie

Civil Service Cricket Club: www.civilservicecc.com

Cycling Ireland: www.cyclingireland.ie

Dublin Zoo: www.dublinzoo.ie

Deer Study Group: www.ucd.ie/zoology

Department of Defence: www.defence.ie

Donore Harriers: www.donoreharriers.com

FAI: www.fai.ie

Farmleigh: www.farmleigh.ie

GAA: www.gaa.ie

Garda Headquarters: www.garda.ie

Garda Museum: www.esatclear.ie/~garda

Motorsport Ireland: www.motorsportireland.com

OPW: www.opw.ie

Phoenix Cricket Club: www.phoenixcricketclub.com

Polo: www.allirelandpoloclub.com

Phoenix Park updates: www.liffey-i.com/phoenixpark.htm

Royal Dublin Fusiliers Association: www.greatwar.ie

US Embassy: http://dublin.usembassy.gov/ireland/Residence.html

INDEX

(Numbers in italics refer to illustrations)